MW00892214

THE SUPER EASY HEART HEALTHY DIET COOKBOOK

1500 Days of Balanced Dining Bliss with a 28-Day Meal Plan to Care for Your Heart | Full Color Edition

Wendy C. Thomas

Copyright© 2024 By Wendy C. Thomas Rights Reserved

This book is copyright protected. It is only for personal use. You cannot amend, distribute, sell, use, quote or paraphrase any part of the content within this book, without the consent of the author or publisher.

Under no circumstances will any blame or legal responsibility be held against the publisher, or author, for any damages, reparation, or monetary loss due to the information contained within this book, either directly or indirectly.

Limit of Liability/Disclaimer of Warranty:

No book, including this one, can ever replace the diagnostic expertise and medical advice of a physician in providing information about your health. The information contained herein is not intended to replace medical advice. You should consult with your doctor before using the information in this or any health-related book.

The Publisher and the author make no representations or warranties with respect to the accuracy or completeness of the contents of this work and specifically disclaim all warranties, including without limitation warranties of fitness for a particular purpose. No warranty may be created or extended by sales or promotional materials. The advice and strategies contained herein may not be suitable for every situation. This work is sold with the understanding that the Publisher is not engaged in rendering medical, legal, or other professional advice or services. If professional assistance is required, the services of a competent professional person should be sought. Neither the Publisher nor the author shall be liable for damages arising herefrom. The fact that an individual, organization, or website is referred to in this work as a citation and/or potential source of further information does not mean that the author or the Publisher endorses the information the individual, organization, or website may provide or recommendations they/it may make. Further, readers should be aware that websites listed in this work may have changed or disappeared between when this work was written and when it is read.

Manufactured in the United States of America

Interior and Cover Designer: Danielle Rees

Art Producer: Brooke White

Editor: Aaliyah Lyons

Production Editor: Sienna Adams

Production Manager: Sarah Johnson

Photography: Michael Smith

TABLE OF CONTENTS

TABLE OF CONTENTS

INTRODUCTION

My journey with the heart healthy diet unfolded in a way I never expected. It all began when I found myself at a professional crossroads, dedicating my life to the health of others yet neglecting my own. As a dietitian, my days were consumed by the science of nutrition and the well-being of my patients, but at home, my personal diet was a reflection of convenience over quality. This dichotomy between my professional beliefs and personal practices was unsettling, and it became a catalyst for change.

The turning point came five years ago during a routine health check. The numbers weren't alarming, but they were a wake-up call. I realized that to truly advocate for heart health, I needed to embody the principles I preached. Thus, I embarked on a personal journey to integrate the heart healthy diet into my life, not just as a dietitian but as Wendy, a person seeking balance and wellness.

Adopting a heart-healthy lifestyle amidst a busy schedule and family responsibilities was daunting at first. The challenge wasn't just about choosing the right foods; it was about redefining what mealtime looked like for us. It meant finding the joy in preparing meals that were not only nutritious but also delicious and satisfying. I started experimenting with recipes, incorporating more plant-based meals, and focusing on whole foods. This wasn't a diet in the traditional sense but a transformation of our family's eating habits.

This personal commitment to heart-healthy eating opened up a new avenue for connection with my clients. I wasn't just advising them based on clinical evidence; I was sharing insights from my own life. This authenticity bridged the gap between practitioner and patient, creating a space for more meaningful conversations about lifestyle changes.

One of the most profound realizations from this journey was understanding the power of small, sustainable changes. I learned that heart health is not about drastic overhauls but about making more healthful choices consistently over time. This principle became a cornerstone of my practice and my personal philosophy.

Today, my relationship with food and heart health is more holistic. It's about nourishing not just the body but the soul, finding pleasure in the simplicity of a home-cooked meal, and the satisfaction of knowing you're taking care of your heart. My family's journey has also evolved; what started as my personal mission has become a collective adventure. We explore new foods together, enjoy the process of cooking, and cherish our mealtime as an opportunity to connect and share.

My story with the heart healthy diet is not just about dietary changes; it's a narrative of personal growth, professional integrity, and the discovery of a deeper passion for nurturing health through food. It reflects the journey of someone who learned that the heart of wellness lies in the balance between what we know and how we live, inspiring others to embark on their own path to heart health.

DEDICATION

To Sarah, whose wisdom has been a guiding light in both my career and my journey as an author. Your insights as a fellow dietitian have sharpened my focus and enriched my pages more than words can express. Beyond the professional realm, your friendship has been a sanctuary, caring for my well-being with a warmth and sincerity that's rare. Your laughter has lightened my heaviest days, and your advice has steered me through countless storms. Here's to the countless meals we've shared and the many more to come. Thank you for being an irreplaceable part of my story.

CHAPTER 1: THE EASY GUIDE TO HEART HEALTH

HEART-HEALTHY DIET ESSENTIALS

In today's world, where heart disease remains a leading cause of mortality, cultivating a heart-healthy diet is essential for promoting overall well-being and longevity. A heart-healthy diet encompasses a balanced and thoughtful approach to eating, emphasizing nutrient-dense foods while minimizing those high in unhealthy fats, sodium, and added sugars. Let's explore in detail what constitutes a heart-healthy diet, what foods to prioritize for heart health, and which ones to limit or avoid to mitigate cardiovascular risk factors.

WHAT IS A HEART-HEALTHY DIET?

A heart-healthy diet is characterized by an abundance of whole, minimally processed foods that provide essential nutrients without excess unhealthy additives. It focuses on incorporating a variety of nutrient-dense foods while limiting those high in saturated fats, trans fats, sodium, and added sugars. By embracing a heart-healthy diet, individuals can nourish their bodies with the nutrients needed to support cardiovascular health, lower cholesterol levels, manage blood pressure, and reduce inflammation—all crucial factors in preventing heart disease.

WHAT TO EAT FOR HEART HEALTH

- **Fruits and Vegetables:** Colorful fruits and vegetables are packed with vitamins, minerals, antioxidants, and dietary fiber, all of which contribute to heart health. Aim to include a diverse array of fruits and vegetables in your diet, incorporating them into meals and snacks to boost your intake of essential nutrients and promote overall well-being.

- **Whole Grains:** Whole grains, such as oats, brown rice, quinoa, barley, and whole wheat, are rich in fiber, vitamins, minerals, and antioxidants. Consuming whole grains regularly can help lower cholesterol levels, regulate blood sugar levels, and reduce the risk of heart disease.

- **Healthy Fats:** Incorporate sources of healthy fats, such as avocados, nuts, seeds, and fatty fish like salmon and mackerel, into your diet. These foods provide omega-3 fatty acids, which have been shown to reduce inflammation, lower triglyceride levels, and improve heart health.

- **Lean Proteins:** Choose lean sources of protein, such as poultry, fish, legumes, tofu, tempeh, and low-fat dairy products. These protein sources are lower in saturated fats compared to red and processed meats, making them heart-healthy choices that can help reduce the risk of cardiovascular disease.

- **Low-Fat Dairy:** Opt for low-fat or fat-free dairy products, such as yogurt, milk, and cheese, to limit saturated fat intake while still obtaining essential nutrients like calcium and protein. Incorporating low-fat dairy options into your diet can support bone health and overall cardiovascular wellness.

FOODS TO LIMIT OR AVOID

- **Saturated and Trans Fats:** Limit consumption of foods high in saturated fats, including red and processed meats, full-fat dairy products, butter, lard, and tropical oils like coconut and palm oil. Additionally, avoid trans fats found in processed and fried foods, as they can raise LDL (bad) cholesterol levels and increase the risk of heart disease.

- **Added Sugars:** Minimize intake of foods and beverages high in added sugars, such as sugary drinks, desserts, candies, pastries, and processed snacks. Excessive sugar consumption can contribute to weight gain, insulin resistance, inflammation, and an increased risk of heart disease.

- **Sodium:** Reduce sodium intake by limiting processed and packaged foods, which are often high in salt. Be mindful of condiments, sauces, canned soups, and pre-packaged meals, as they may contain hidden sources of sodium. Opt for fresh or minimally processed foods and use herbs, spices, and citrus juices to flavor dishes instead of salt.

- **Refined Carbohydrates:** Limit consumption of refined carbohydrates, including white bread, white rice, pasta, pastries, and sugary cereals. These foods are high in refined sugars and can cause spikes in blood sugar levels, leading to insulin resistance and an increased risk of heart disease.

SMART SHOPPING TIPS

Smart shopping is a cornerstone of maintaining a heart-healthy diet. By making informed choices at the grocery store, you can stock your kitchen with nutritious foods that support cardiovascular wellness while minimizing the intake of unhealthy options. In this comprehensive guide, we'll explore practical strategies and tips for smart shopping to help you navigate the aisles with confidence and prioritize foods that promote heart health.

PLAN BEFORE YOU SHOP

CREATE A SHOPPING LIST

Start by planning your meals for the week and creating a detailed shopping list based on your menu. This not only helps you stay organized but also prevents impulse purchases of unhealthy items.

CHECK YOUR PANTRY

Take inventory of what you already have at home to avoid duplicate purchases and ensure you have essential staples on hand for meal preparation.

SET A BUDGET

Establish a budget for your shopping trip to help you make cost-effective choices

and avoid overspending. Look for sales, discounts, and coupons to maximize your savings without compromising on quality.

CHOOSE NUTRIENT-DENSE FOODS

DARK LEAFY GREENS (SPINACH, KALE, SWISS CHARD):

- Rich in vitamins A, C, and K, folate, iron, and fiber.
- These greens provide essential nutrients crucial for heart health, including antioxidants, which help combat inflammation and oxidative stress.

FATTY FISH (SALMON, MACKEREL):

- High in omega-3 fatty acids.
- Omega-3 fatty acids are known for their anti-inflammatory properties, reducing the risk of heart disease and promoting overall cardiovascular health.

COLORFUL BERRIES (BLUEBERRIES, STRAWBERRIES, RASPBERRIES):

- Rich in antioxidants and fiber.
- Berries contain phytonutrients like flavonoids and anthocyanins, which help protect against oxidative damage and inflammation, supporting heart health.

WHOLE GRAINS (QUINOA, BROWN RICE):

- Provide complex carbohydrates, fiber, and essential nutrients.
- Whole grains offer sustained energy release, promote digestive health, and help regulate blood sugar levels, all of which contribute to heart health.

READ LABELS WISELY

CHECK THE NUTRITION FACTS PANEL

Pay attention to serving sizes, calories, and nutrient content per serving when comparing products. Look for foods low in saturated fats, trans fats, sodium, and added sugars, and high in fiber, vitamins, and minerals.

SCAN THE INGREDIENT LIST

Read the ingredient list to identify hidden sources of unhealthy additives like hydrogenated oils, high-fructose corn syrup, artificial flavors, and preservatives. Choose products with minimal, recognizable ingredients and avoid those with long lists of additives and artificial additives.

NAVIGATE THE AISLES MINDFULLY

- **Shop the Perimeter:** Start your shopping trip on the perimeter of the store, where fresh produce, meats, dairy, and whole foods are typically located. This helps you prioritize nutrient-dense options and avoid the temptation of processed and unhealthy foods found in the center aisles.

- **Beware of Marketing Tactics:** Be cautious of health claims and marketing tactics that may be misleading. Just because a product is labeled as "low-fat" or "all-natural" doesn't necessarily mean it's a healthy choice. Always read the nutrition label and ingredient list to make informed decisions.

STOCK UP ON HEALTHY STAPLES

- **Bulk Up on Beans and Legumes:** Beans and legumes are excellent sources of plant-based protein, fiber, vitamins, and minerals. Stock up on dried or canned beans and lentils to incorporate into soups, salads, stews, and grain bowls for added nutrition and satiety.

- **Invest in Healthy Snacks:** Choose nutrient-dense snacks like fresh fruit, raw vegetables, nuts, seeds, yogurt,

and whole grain crackers to keep on hand for quick and convenient options between meals. Avoid processed snacks high in refined sugars, unhealthy fats, and artificial additives.

VITAL COOKING TECHNIQUES

In the journey toward heart health, the way we prepare our food plays a crucial role. By utilizing cooking techniques that preserve nutrients and minimize the use of unhealthy fats, sugars, and sodium, we can create delicious meals that support cardiovascular wellness. Let's explore some vital cooking techniques for heart health and understand how each one contributes to a nourishing and flavorful diet.

1. GRILLING

Grilling is a popular cooking technique that adds a smoky flavor to foods without the need for excessive fats or oils. When grilling meats, opt for lean cuts like skinless poultry, fish, or trimmed beef to minimize saturated fat intake. Marinating meats with herbs, spices, and citrus juices before grilling can add flavor without the need for excess salt or high-calorie sauces. Additionally, grilling vegetables enhances their natural sweetness and preserves their nutrients, making them a heart-healthy addition to any meal.

2. BAKING

Baking is a gentle cooking method that requires little to no added fats, making it ideal for heart-healthy cooking. When baking meats, poultry, or fish, use a baking rack to allow excess fat to drain away during cooking, reducing the overall fat content of the dish. Baking vegetables at a moderate temperature helps retain their nutrients while caramelizing their natural sugars, resulting in delicious and nutritious side dishes. For baked goods, opt for recipes that use whole grains, natural sweeteners like honey or maple syrup, and heart-healthy fats like olive oil or mashed avocado.

3. STEAMING

Steaming is a simple and effective cooking technique that preserves the natural flavors and nutrients of foods without the need for added fats. Steaming vegetables, seafood, and poultry helps retain their texture and color while reducing the risk of nutrient loss compared to boiling or frying. To steam foods, simply place them in a steamer basket or on a rack over simmering water and cover tightly to trap steam. Steamed dishes can be seasoned with herbs, spices, and citrus zest to enhance flavor without added salt or unhealthy fats.

4. SAUTEING

Sauteing involves cooking foods quickly in a small amount of oil over high heat, making it a convenient and versatile cooking technique. When sauteing, choose heart-healthy oils like olive, avocado, or coconut oil, which are high in monounsaturated fats and have been shown to improve cholesterol levels. Use a non-stick skillet to minimize the need for excess oil and prevent foods from sticking.

Sauteing vegetables, lean proteins, and whole grains with aromatic herbs and spices creates flavorful dishes that are both satisfying and heart-healthy.

5. ROASTING

Roasting is a dry-heat cooking method that intensifies the natural flavors of foods while caramelizing their sugars for a rich and savory taste. When roasting meats, poultry, or vegetables, use a moderate amount of heart-healthy oil or cooking spray to prevent sticking and promote browning. Roasting root vegetables like sweet potatoes, carrots, and beets enhances their sweetness and creates a satisfying side dish or salad topping. For added flavor, season roasted dishes with herbs, spices, and citrus zest before serving.

6. POACHING

Poaching involves gently simmering foods in liquid until they are cooked through, resulting in tender and flavorful dishes. Poaching is particularly well-suited for delicate proteins like fish, chicken breasts, and eggs, as well as fruits like pears and apples. When poaching, use low-sodium broths or aromatic liquids like wine, citrus juice, or herbal teas to infuse foods with flavor without excess salt or fat. Poached dishes can be served hot or cold and are easily customizable with a variety of herbs, spices, and sauces.

In conclusion, the path to heart health begins with understanding the importance of nutrition, lifestyle, and mindful cooking. By prioritizing nutrient-dense foods, adopting smart shopping strategies, and mastering wholesome cooking techniques, we empower ourselves to make informed choices that support cardiovascular wellness. Through small, intentional changes in our daily habits, we can cultivate a lifestyle that nurtures our hearts and promotes overall well-being. As we embark on this journey together, let us embrace the opportunity to nourish ourselves with delicious, heart-healthy meals that not only satisfy our taste buds but also nourish our bodies and minds. With dedication and commitment, we can build a foundation for lifelong vitality and happiness.

CHAPTER 2: 4-WEEK MEAL PLAN

WEEK 1

Day 1:

Breakfast: **Potato, Pepper, and Egg Breakfast Casserole**

Lunch: **Turkey Meatballs**

Snack: **Happy Heart Energy Bites**

Dinner: **Baked Salmon Dijon**

Total for the day:

Calories: 900; Fat: 39g; Carbs: 61g; Fiber: 8g; Protein: 80g

Day 2:

Breakfast: **Potato, Pepper, and Egg Breakfast Casserole**

Lunch: **Turkey Meatballs**

Snack: **Happy Heart Energy Bites**

Dinner: **Baked Salmon Dijon**

Total for the day:

Calories: 900; Fat: 39g; Carbs: 61g; Fiber: 8g; Protein: 80g

Day 3:

Breakfast: **Potato, Pepper, and Egg Breakfast Casserole**

Lunch: **Turkey Meatballs**

Snack: **Happy Heart Energy Bites**

Dinner: **Baked Salmon Dijon**

Total for the day:

Calories: 900; Fat: 39g; Carbs: 61g; Fiber: 8g; Protein: 80g

Day 4:

Breakfast: **Potato, Pepper, and Egg Breakfast Casserole**

Lunch: **Turkey Meatballs**

Snack: **Happy Heart Energy Bites**

Dinner: **Baked Salmon Dijon**

Total for the day:

Calories: 900; Fat: 39g; Carbs: 61g; Fiber: 8g; Protein: 80g

Day 5:

Breakfast: **Potato, Pepper, and Egg Breakfast Casserole**

Lunch: **Turkey Meatballs**

Snack: **Happy Heart Energy Bites**

Dinner: **Baked Salmon Dijon**

Total for the day:

Calories: 900; Fat: 39g; Carbs: 61g; Fiber: 8g; Protein: 80g

Day 6:

Breakfast: **Potato, Pepper, and Egg Breakfast Casserole**

Lunch: **Nature's Veggie Burger**

Snack: **Happy Heart Energy Bites**

Dinner: **Nature's Veggie Burger**

Total for the day:

Calories: 1011; Fat: 49g; Carbs: 82g; Fiber: 11g; Protein: 59g

Day 7:

Breakfast: **Potato, Pepper, and Egg Breakfast Casserole**

Lunch: **Nature's Veggie Burger**

Snack: **Happy Heart Energy Bites**

Dinner: **Nature's Veggie Burger**

Total for the day:

Calories: 1011; Fat: 49g; Carbs: 82g; Fiber: 11g; Protein: 59g

WEEK 2

Day 1:

Breakfast: Mini Banana Vegan Muffins

Lunch: Lamb Roast with Root Vegetables

Snack: Sour Cream Green Beans

Dinner: Shredded Chicken Sloppy Joes

Total for the day:

Calories: 1189; Fat: 35.7g; Carbs: 135.3g; Fiber: 21g; Protein: 94g

Day 2:

Breakfast: Mini Banana Vegan Muffins

Lunch: Lamb Roast with Root Vegetables

Snack: Sour Cream Green Beans

Dinner: Shredded Chicken Sloppy Joes

Total for the day:

Calories: 1189; Fat: 35.7g; Carbs: 135.3g; Fiber: 21g; Protein: 94g

Day 3:

Breakfast: Mini Banana Vegan Muffins

Lunch: Lamb Roast with Root Vegetables

Snack: Sour Cream Green Beans

Dinner: Shredded Chicken Sloppy Joes

Total for the day:

Calories: 1189; Fat: 35.7g; Carbs: 135.3g; Fiber: 21g; Protein: 94g

Day 4:

Breakfast: Mini Banana Vegan Muffins

Lunch: Lamb Roast with Root Vegetables

Snack: Sour Cream Green Beans

Dinner: Shredded Chicken Sloppy Joes

Total for the day:

Calories: 1189; Fat: 35.7g; Carbs: 135.3g; Fiber: 21g; Protein: 94g

Day 5:

Breakfast: Mini Banana Vegan Muffins

Lunch: Lamb Roast with Root Vegetables

Snack: Sour Cream Green Beans

Dinner: Shredded Chicken Sloppy Joes

Total for the day:

Calories: 1189; Fat: 35.7g; Carbs: 135.3g; Fiber: 21g; Protein: 94g

Day 6:

Breakfast: Mini Banana Vegan Muffins

Lunch: Lamb Roast with Root Vegetables

Snack: Sour Cream Green Beans

Dinner: Shredded Chicken Sloppy Joes

Total for the day:

Calories: 1189; Fat: 35.7g; Carbs: 135.3g; Fiber: 21g; Protein: 94g

Day 7:

Breakfast: Mini Banana Vegan Muffins

Lunch: Lamb Roast with Root Vegetables

Snack: Sour Cream Green Beans

Dinner: Shredded Chicken Sloppy Joes

Total for the day:

Calories: 1189; Fat: 35.7g; Carbs: 135.3g; Fiber: 21g; Protein: 94g

WEEK 3

Day 1:

Breakfast: Stacked Sausage and Eggs

Lunch: Italian-Style Tuna Salad

Snack: Fall-Spiced Applesauce

Dinner: Citrusy Mexican Pulled Pork

Total for the day:

Calories: 676; Fat: 27g; Carbs: 55g; Fiber: 9g; Protein: 61g

Day 2:

Breakfast: Stacked Sausage and Eggs

Lunch: Italian-Style Tuna Salad

Snack: Fall-Spiced Applesauce

Dinner: Citrusy Mexican Pulled Pork

Total for the day:

Calories: 676; Fat: 27g; Carbs: 55g; Fiber: 9g; Protein: 61g

Day 3:

Breakfast: Stacked Sausage and Eggs

Lunch: Italian-Style Tuna Salad

Snack: Fall-Spiced Applesauce

Dinner: Citrusy Mexican Pulled Pork

Total for the day:

Calories: 676; Fat: 27g; Carbs: 55g; Fiber: 9g; Protein: 61g

Day 4:

Breakfast: Stacked Sausage and Eggs

Lunch: Italian-Style Tuna Salad

Snack: Fall-Spiced Applesauce

Dinner: Citrusy Mexican Pulled Pork

Total for the day:

Calories: 676; Fat: 27g; Carbs: 55g; Fiber: 9g; Protein: 61g

Day 5:

Breakfast: Salmon and Avocado Toast

Lunch: Green Beans Sauté

Snack: Fall-Spiced Applesauce

Dinner: Citrusy Mexican Pulled Pork

Total for the day:

Calories: 813; Fat: 33g; Carbs: 80g; Fiber: 16g; Protein: 59g

Day 6:

Breakfast: Salmon and Avocado Toast

Lunch: Green Beans Sauté

Snack: Fall-Spiced Applesauce

Dinner: Citrusy Mexican Pulled Pork

Total for the day:

Calories: 813; Fat: 33g; Carbs: 80g; Fiber: 16g; Protein: 59g

Day 7:

Breakfast: Salmon and Avocado Toast

Lunch: Green Beans Sauté

Snack: Fall-Spiced Applesauce

Dinner: Green Beans Sauté

Total for the day:

Calories: 634; Fat: 26g; Carbs: 81g; Fiber: 17g; Protein: 32g

WEEK 4

Day 1:

Breakfast: **Blueberry-Walnut Steel-Cut Oatmeal**

Lunch: **Marinated Steak**

Snack: **Strawberry-Raspberry Ice**

Dinner: **Sesame Soy Chicken**

Total for the day:

Calories: **666**; Fat: **17g**; Carbs: **72g**; Fiber: **7g**; Protein: **57g**

Day 2:

Breakfast: **Blueberry-Walnut Steel-Cut Oatmeal**

Lunch: **Marinated Steak**

Snack: **Strawberry-Raspberry Ice**

Dinner: **Sesame Soy Chicken**

Total for the day:

Calories: **666**; Fat: **17g**; Carbs: **72g**; Fiber: **7g**; Protein: **57g**

Day 3:

Breakfast: **Blueberry-Walnut Steel-Cut Oatmeal**

Lunch: **Marinated Steak**

Snack: **Strawberry-Raspberry Ice**

Dinner: **Sesame Soy Chicken**

Total for the day:

Calories: **666**; Fat: **17g**; Carbs: **72g**; Fiber: **7g**; Protein: **57g**

Day 4:

Breakfast: **Blueberry-Walnut Steel-Cut Oatmeal**

Lunch: **Marinated Steak**

Snack: **Strawberry-Raspberry Ice**

Dinner: **Sesame Soy Chicken**

Total for the day:

Calories: **666**; Fat: **17g**; Carbs: **72g**; Fiber: **7g**; Protein: **57g**

Day 5:

Breakfast: **Blueberry-Walnut Steel-Cut Oatmeal**

Lunch: **Marinated Steak**

Snack: **Strawberry-Raspberry Ice**

Dinner: **Sesame Soy Chicken**

Total for the day:

Calories: **666**; Fat: **17g**; Carbs: **72g**; Fiber: **7g**; Protein: **57g**

Day 6:

Breakfast: **Blueberry-Walnut Steel-Cut Oatmeal**

Lunch: **Marinated Steak**

Snack: **Strawberry-Raspberry Ice**

Dinner: **Sesame Soy Chicken**

Total for the day:

Calories: **666**; Fat: **17g**; Carbs: **72g**; Fiber: **7g**; Protein: **57g**

Day 7:

Breakfast: **Blueberry-Walnut Steel-Cut Oatmeal**

Lunch: **Roasted Summer Squash Farro Salad**

Snack: **Strawberry-Raspberry Ice**

Dinner: **Roasted Summer Squash Farro Salad**

Total for the day:

Calories: **743**; Fat: **26g**; Carbs: **115g**; Fiber: **20g**; Protein: **22g**

CHAPTER 3:
SEASONINGS DELIGHTS

YOGURT-HERB DRESSING

Prep time: 10 minutes | Cook time: 10 minutes | Makes 1¼ cups

- 1 cup plain, unsweetened, low-fat greek yogurt
- ¼ cup chopped fresh chives
- ¼ cup chopped fresh parsley
- 2 tablespoons extra-virgin olive oil
- 2 tablespoons rice vinegar
- 2 garlic cloves, minced
- ¼ teaspoon salt
- ¼ teaspoon freshly ground black pepper

1. In a small bowl, whisk together the yogurt, chives, parsley, oil, vinegar, garlic, salt, and pepper to combine.
2. Store in an airtight container in the refrigerator for up to 5 days.

Per Serving

Calories: 42 | Total fat: 3g | Saturated fat: 1g | Sodium: 76mg | Carbs: 2g | Fiber: 0g | Protein: 1g

CRANBERRY SAUCE

Prep time: 5 minutes | Cook time: 3 to 4 hours on high or 7 to 8 hours on low | Makes about 1½ cups

- 12 ounces fresh cranberries
- ½ cup 100% orange juice
- ½ cup water
- ⅓ cup sugar (use your desired kind of sugar or sweetener, add more or less to taste)

1. Combine the ingredients in a 6-quart slow cooker. Cover and cook on high for 3 to 4 hours or on low for 7 to 8 hours, or until the cranberries have popped open and the sauce is bubbly.
2. Taste and stir in any extra sweetener or any other add-ins of your choice, such as orange zest, a pinch of ground ginger, a pinch of cinnamon or cloves, or a splash of vanilla extract. Serve warm.

Per Serving

Calories: 155 | Total Fat: 0g | Saturated Fat: 0g | Sodium: 3mg | Carbs: 40g | Fiber: 5g | Sugars: 30g | Protein: 1g

BLUEBERRY SAUCE

Prep time: **10 minutes** | Cook time: **4 minutes** | Serves **6**

- 1 pint blueberries or 2 cups frozen unsweetened blueberries
- ½ cup water
- ¼ cup sugar
- 1 tablespoon fresh lemon juice
- 1 tablespoon cornstarch
- 2 tablespoons cold water

1. In a medium saucepan over medium-high heat, bring the blueberries, water, sugar, and lemon juice to a boil. If using fresh blueberries, reduce the heat and simmer for 1 to 2 minutes, or until softened. If using frozen berries, there's no need to simmer.
2. In a small bowl, stir together the cornstarch and water until the cornstarch is dissolved. Stir into the blueberry mixture. Reduce the heat to low. Cook for 1 to 2 minutes, stirring until thick and smooth. Serve hot or cold.

Per Serving

Calories: **66** | Total Fat: **0.0 g** | Saturated Fat: **0.0 g** | Sodium: **2 mg** | Carbs: **17 gg** | Fiber: **1 g** | Protein: **0 g**

MARINARA SAUCE

Prep time: **5 minutes** | Cook time: **20 minutes** | Makes **about 2 cups**

- 2 tablespoons extra-virgin olive oil
- 1 onion, chopped
- 2 garlic cloves, minced
- 1 (28-ounce) can whole tomatoes
- 1 thyme sprig
- 2 tablespoons chopped fresh basil leaves

1. In a large saucepan, heat the oil over medium-high heat.
2. Add the onion, and sauté for 3 to 5 minutes, or until softened and lightly browned.
3. Add the garlic, and cook for 30 seconds, or until fragrant.
4. Add the tomatoes with their juices, breaking them up using a spoon as you mix.
5. Add the thyme, and simmer for 10 minutes, or until the flavors meld. Remove from the heat.
6. Top with the basil.

Per Serving

Calories: **52** | Total fat: **4g** | Saturated fat: **1g** | Sodium: **115mg** | Carbs: **5g** | Fiber: **2g** | Protein: **1g**

LEMON DRESSING

Prep time: **10 minutes** | Cook time: **none** | Serves **8**

- ½ cup fresh lemon juice (about 2 large lemons)
- 2 tablespoons water
- 1 tablespoon chopped fresh parsley
- 1 tablespoon chopped fresh oregano
- 1 tablespoon olive oil (extra-virgin preferred)
- 1 tablespoon honey
- 1 tablespoon Dijon mustard (lowest sodium available)
- 2 medium garlic cloves, minced
- ½ teaspoon fennel seeds, crushed

1. In a small glass bowl, whisk together all the ingredients. Cover and refrigerate for up to three days.
2. Cook's Tip on Fennel: Known primarily as an Italian spice and herb, fennel has a delicate anise flavor. The two main kinds of fennel both have feathery fronds and celery-like stems. Garden, or common, fennel produces the fennel seed that's used as a spice. Fennel seeds resemble caraway seeds and are usually ground before they're used. Florence fennel, or finocchio, is prized for the thickened leaf stalks that form a bulb at the base.
3. The bulb and stems of both kinds can be used as a vegetable, raw or cooked, much as celery is used. The fronds can be chopped and used for flavoring. Add them to cooked dishes at the last minute so the flavor doesn't dissipate.

Per Serving

Calories: **31** | Total Fat: **2.0 g** | Saturated Fat: **0.0 g** |Sodium: **39 mg** | Carbs: **4 gg** | Fiber: **0 g** | Protein: **0 g**

RASPBERRY-TARRAGON VINAIGRETTE

Prep time: **5 minutes** | Cook time: **12 minutes** | Makes **½ cup**

- ½ cup fresh raspberries (do not use frozen; see tip)
- 2 tablespoons white wine vinegar
- 1 clove garlic, minced
- 1 tablespoon minced shallot
- 1 teaspoon honey
- ⅛ teaspoon salt
- 2 tablespoons extra-virgin olive oil
- 1 teaspoon dried tarragon

1. In a blender or food processor, puree the raspberries, vinegar, garlic, shallot, honey, and salt. Pour into a small bowl.
2. Add the olive oil in a thin stream while whisking constantly. Stir in the tarragon.
3. Use immediately or store in an airtight container in the refrigerator for up to 2 days.

Per serving

Calories: **48** | Total fat: **4 g** | Saturated fat: **<1 g** | Sodium: **73 mg** | Total Carbs: **4 g** | Fiber: **1 g** | Protein: **<1 g**

CHAPTER 4: BREAKFAST BONANZA

OMEGA-3 SKILLET GRANOLA

Prep time: **10 minutes** | Cook time: **10 minutes** | Serves **4**

- 2 tablespoons better butter or 1 tablespoon canola or sunflower oil plus 1 tablespoon unsalted butter
- 1 tablespoon honey
- ¾ cup large-flake rolled oats
- ⅓ cup roughly chopped walnuts
- 1 tablespoon chia seeds
- 1 tablespoon hemp seeds
- 1 tablespoon ground flaxseed
- ½ teaspoon ground cinnamon
- pinch salt

1. In a large skillet, melt the Better Butter and honey over medium heat, then continue to cook until bubbly.
2. Stir in the oats, walnuts, chia seeds, hemp seeds, flaxseed, cinnamon, and salt and cook, stirring, until the oats and nuts start to brown, 3 to 4 minutes. If they're browning too fast, turn the heat down to medium-low.
3. Eat the granola right away or let it cool completely, then store in an airtight container for up to 2 weeks in the pantry or 3 months in the freezer.

Per Serving

Calories: **230** | Total Fat: **16g** | Saturated Fat: **3g** | Sodium: **64mg** | Carbs: **18g** | Fiber: **4g** | Protein: **5g** |

BLUEBERRY-WALNUT STEEL-CUT OATMEAL

Prep time: **5 minutes** | Cook time: **7 to 8 hours on low** | Serves **8**

- nonstick cooking spray
- 2 cups steel-cut oats
- 6 cups water
- 2 cups low-fat or fat-free milk, or plant-based milk
- 2 cups fresh or frozen blueberries
- 1 ripe banana, mashed
- 1 teaspoon vanilla extract
- 2 teaspoons ground cinnamon
- 2 tablespoons brown sugar
- pinch salt
- ½ cup chopped walnuts, for garnish

1. Spray the bowl of the slow cooker with the cooking spray.
2. Place the oats, water, milk, blueberries, banana, vanilla, cinnamon, brown sugar, and salt in the slow cooker. Stir well. Cover and cook on low for 7 to 8 hours.
3. Serve warm garnished with the chopped walnuts.

Per Serving

Calories: **202** | Total Fat: **4g** | Saturated Fat: **1g** | Sodium: **95mg** | Carbs: **36g** | Fiber: **4g** | Protein: **8g**

CHERRY-NUT BREAD

Prep time: 10 minutes | Cook time: 40 minutes | Serves 16

- Cooking spray
- 2 cups white whole-wheat flour
- ½ cup firmly packed light brown sugar
- 2 teaspoons baking powder
- ¼ teaspoon salt
- ¼ teaspoon baking soda
- 1 cup fat-free milk
- ¼ cup egg substitute
- 1 teaspoon grated orange zest
- ½ cup chopped almonds, dry-roasted
- ½ cup dried cherries

1. Preheat the oven to 350°F. Lightly spray an 8 ½ × 4 ½ × 2 ½-inch loaf pan with cooking spray.
2. In a large bowl, sift together the flour, brown sugar, baking powder, salt, and baking soda.
3. In a separate large bowl, whisk together the milk, egg substitute, and orange zest.
4. Add the flour mixture, almonds, and cherries to the milk mixture. Stir just until the dry ingredients are moistened but no flour is visible. Don't overmix; the batter should be slightly lumpy. Pour into the loaf pan, gently smoothing the top.
5. Bake for 40 minutes, or until a wooden toothpick inserted in the center comes out clean. Using a metal spatula, loosen the bread from the sides of the pan. Turn out onto a cooling rack. Let cool before slicing.

Per Serving

Calories: **117** | Total Fat: **2.0 g** | Saturated Fat: **0.0 g** | Sodium: **122 mg** | Carbs: **21 gg** | Fiber: **2 g** | Protein: **4 g**

MINI BANANA VEGAN MUFFINS

Prep time: 5 minutes | Cook time: 18 minutes | Serves 8

- ½ cup whole wheat flour
- ¼ cup all-purpose flour
- ½ teaspoon baking soda
- /2 teaspoon baking powder
- ½ teaspoon ground cinnamon
- 1/8 teaspoon salt
- 2 medium ripe bananas
- ¼ cup firmly packed brown sugar
- ⅛ cup unsweetened applesauce
- ⅛ teaspoon vanilla extract
- 1 ½ tablespoons extra virgin olive oil
- ¼ cup toasted chopped walnuts

1. Preheat the oven to 375°F. Spray a mini muffin pan with olive oil spray.
2. In a large bowl, sift together the flours, baking soda, baking powder, cinnamon, and salt. In a separate large bowl, mash the bananas, and add the brown sugar, applesauce, vanilla, and oil. Stir the flour mixture into the banana mixture just until moistened. Do not overstir the batter. Fold in the walnuts.
3. Using a teaspoon, spoon the batter into the prepared muffin cups. Bake for 15 to 18 minutes, or until a toothpick inserted into center of a muffin comes out clean. Do not overbake.

Per Serving

Calories:**188** | Total Fat:**7 g** | Saturated Fat:**0.9 g** | Total Carbs:**34 g** | Fiber:**3 g** | Protein:**3 g**

POTATO, PEPPER, AND EGG BREAKFAST CASSEROLE

Prep time: **10 minutes** | Cook time: **7 to 8 hours on low** | Serves 8

- 12 large eggs
- 1 cup low-fat milk
- ¼ teaspoon dried mustard
- ½ teaspoon garlic powder
- ½ teaspoon salt
- ½ teaspoon freshly ground black pepper
- nonstick cooking spray
- 1 (30-ounce) bag frozen hash browns, thawed in the refrigerator
- 1 (14-ounce) bag frozen peppers and onions, thawed in the refrigerator
- 6 ounces (1½ cups) 2% shredded cheddar cheese

1. In a large bowl, whisk together the eggs, milk, dried mustard, garlic powder, salt, and pepper.
2. Spray the bowl a 6-quart slow cooker with the cooking spray. Layer one-third of the hash browns in the slow cooker followed by one-third of the peppers and onions, then one-third of the cheese. Repeat the layers two more times.
3. Slowly pour the egg mixture over the top. Cover and cook on low for 7 to 8 hours.
4. Cut into 8 wedges and serve hot.

Per Serving

Calories: **340** | Total Fat: **18g** | Saturated Fat: **6g** | Carbs: **27g** | Fiber: **3g** | Sugars: **3g** | Protein: **20g**

SALMON AND AVOCADO TOAST

Prep time: **15 minutes** | Cook time: **15 minutes** | Serves 3

- 1½ whole-grain bagels, split
- 1 (7.6-ounce) can sockeye salmon, drained
- 1 tablespoon extra-virgin olive oil
- 1 avocado, peeled and pitted
- 1 tablespoon freshly squeezed lime juice
- ½ cup chopped fresh tomatoes
- ¼ cup minced red onion (optional)
- freshly ground black pepper (optional)

1. Toast the bagels.
2. Meanwhile, in a medium bowl, mix the salmon with the olive oil, breaking up the pieces.
3. In a small bowl, mash the avocado with the lime juice.
4. Top each toasted bagel half with some salmon mix. Spread the avocado on top of the salmon, followed by the tomatoes, then onion and pepper (if using).

Per Serving

Calories: **366** | Total Fat: **18g** | Saturated Fat: **3g** | Sodium: **463mg** | Carbs: **27g** | Fiber: **7g** | Protein: **27g**

STACKED SAUSAGE AND EGGS

Prep time: **10 minutes** | Cook time: **8 minutes** |
Serves **4**

- 4 ounces low-fat bulk sausage
- 2 to 3 ounces button mushrooms, sliced
- ½ large onion, chopped
- ½ medium green bell pepper, chopped
- 1 cup egg substitute
- 3 tablespoons fat-free milk
- ⅛ teaspoon cayenne
- 2 tablespoons chopped fresh parsley
- ⅛ teaspoon salt

1. In a large nonstick skillet, cook the sausage over medium-high heat for 2 to 3 minutes, or until no longer pink, stirring constantly to turn and break up the sausage. Transfer to a medium bowl.
2. In the same skillet, stir together the mushrooms, onion, and bell pepper. Cook for about 3 minutes, or until the onion is soft, stirring occasionally. Stir into the sausage. Cover to keep warm.
3. Meanwhile, in a small bowl, whisk together the egg substitute, milk, and cayenne.
4. Wipe the skillet with paper towels. Heat the skillet over medium heat. Cook the egg mixture for 2 minutes, stirring frequently. Transfer to plates. Top with the sausage mixture. Sprinkle with the parsley and salt.

Per Serving

Calories: **88** | Total Fat: **1.0g** | Saturated Fat: **0.0g** | Carbs: **66g** | Fiber: **1g** | Protein: **12g**

CHICKPEA AND BRUSSELS SPROUTS HASH

Prep time: **10 minutes** | Cook time: **10 minutes** | Serves **2**

- ½ cup canned chickpeas, reserving 2 tablespoons packing water
- 2 tablespoons water
- ¼ teaspoon freshly ground black pepper
- 1 tablespoon nutritional yeast
- 1 teaspoon chia seeds
- 2 teaspoons avocado oil
- 1 scallion, finely chopped
- 1 cup shaved brussels sprouts

1. In a blender, put the chickpeas, reserved packing water, water, pepper, and nutritional yeast. Blend for 1 to 2 minutes, until the ingredients are well combined but the chickpeas still have some texture. Add the chia seeds to the mixture and let sit for about 5 minutes.
2. In a medium saucepan, heat the oil on medium heat for about 1 minute, until the pan is hot. Then add the chickpea mixture and cook for about 3 minutes, stirring occasionally. Using a spatula, chop the formed mixture in the pan to resemble a hash. Add in the scallion and cook for 1 more minute, until the chickpea mixture is lightly browned.
3. Add the Brussels sprouts, cover, and cook for 2 minutes, until the sprouts become slightly wilted. Divide the mixture in half and serve. Store in the refrigerator in an airtight container for up to 3 days.

Per Serving

Calories: **142** | Total fat: **7g** | Saturated fat: **1g** | Carbs: **16g** | Sugars: **3g** | Fiber: **6g** | Protein: **7g**

CINNAMON-ORANGE PANCAKES

Prep time: **10 minutes** | Cook time: **6 minutes** | Serves **4**

- 1 cup whole-wheat flour
- ¾ cup all-purpose flour
- 2 tablespoons toasted wheat germ
- 1 tablespoon sugar
- 2 teaspoons baking powder
- 1 teaspoon ground cinnamon
- 1 cup fat-free milk
- 1 teaspoon grated orange zest
- ¾ cup fresh orange juice
- ¼ cup egg substitute
- Cooking spray

1. Preheat the oven to 200°F. Place a cooling rack on a baking sheet. Set aside.
2. In a large bowl, stir together the flours, wheat germ, sugar, baking powder, and cinnamon.
3. In a small bowl, whisk together the remaining ingredients except the cooking spray. Pour into the flour mixture. Stir until the flour mixture is moistened but no flour is visible. Don't overmix.
4. Lightly spray a griddle or large skillet with cooking spray. Heat over medium heat. For each pancake, ladle ¼ cup batter onto the griddle. Cook for 2 to 3 minutes, or until bubbles are forming on the top of the pancakes and the edges are dry.
5. Turn over the pancakes. Cook for 2 to 3 minutes. Transfer the pancakes to the cooling rack, placing them in a single layer and leaving space between. Put in the oven to keep warm. Repeat with the remaining batter (you should have a total of 12 pancakes).

Per Serving

Calories: **264** | Total Fat: **1.5 g** | Saturated Fat: **0.5 g** | Sodium: **259 mg** | Carbs: **53 gg** | Fiber: **5 g** | Sugars: **11 g** | Protein: **11 g**

OVERNIGHT CHIA SEED AND COCONUT MILK PUDDING

Prep time: **5 minutes** | Cook time: **none** | Serves **4**

- ½ cup chia seeds
- 2 cups light coconut milk
- 3 teaspoons honey, divided
- ¼ cup sliced banana
- ¼ cup fresh raspberries
- ½ tablespoon sliced almonds
- ½ tablespoon chopped walnuts
- 2 teaspoons unsweetened cocoa powder, divided

1. Mix the chia seeds, coconut milk, and 2 teaspoons of honey together in a small bowl. Portion into two glass Mason jars and refrigerate for 8 hours or overnight.
2. Remove the jars from the refrigerator and top each jar with half the banana, raspberries, almonds, walnuts, and cocoa. Drizzle each jar with the remaining 1 teaspoon of honey, dividing it equally.
3. Enjoy immediately.

Per Serving

Calories: **732** | Fats: **63g** | Protein: **13g** | Cholesterol: **0mg** | Carbs: **41g** | Fiber: **18g** | Sodium: **38mg**

CHAPTER 5: SNACK OASIS

HAPPY HEART ENERGY BITES

Prep time: **20 minutes** | Cook time: **30 minutes** | Serves **30**

- 1 cup rolled oats
- ¾ cup chopped walnuts
- ½ cup natural peanut butter
- ½ cup ground flaxseed
- ¼ cup honey
- ¼ cup dried cranberries

1. Combine the oats, walnuts, peanut butter, flaxseed, honey, and cranberries in a large bowl. Refrigerate for 10 to 20 minutes, if you can, to make them easier to roll.
2. Roll into ¾-inch balls. Store in the fridge or freezer, if they don't disappear first.

Per Serving

Calories: **174** | Total Fat: **10g** | Saturated Fat: **1g** Carbs: **17g** | Fiber: **3g** | **Added** Sugars: **7g** | Protein: **5g**

FRENCH ONION DIP

Prep time: **5 minutes** | Cook time: **none** | Serves **8**

- 2 tablespoons extra virgin olive oil
- 1 small white onion, chopped
- 2 cloves garlic, minced
- 1 cup low-fat plain Greek yogurt
- 1 cup low-fat sour cream
- 2 tablespoons Worcestershire sauce
- ⅛ teaspoon sea salt
- ⅛ teaspoon cracked black pepper
- Minced chives, for garnish

1. Heat the oil in a small pan over low heat. Add the onion and garlic, and sauté until the onion becomes brown and tender. (Keep the heat low, and move the onion minimally to "sweat" it.) Remove from heat.
2. In a separate bowl, combine the yogurt, sour cream, Worcestershire sauce, and salt and pepper to taste. Add the onion and garlic mixture, and mix well. Garnish with minced chives.

Per Serving

Calories:**161** | Total Fat:**12 g** | Saturated Fat:**6 g** |Total Carbs:**9 g** | Fiber:**0.1 g** | Sugars:**6 g** | Protein:**5 g**

BRAISED BELL PEPPERS

Prep time: 15 minutes | Cook time: 10 minutes | Serves 6

- 1 cup onion, sliced
- 3 teaspoons garlic, minced
- 2 tablespoons canola oil
- 8 cups bell peppers, seeded and julienned
- ½ cup low-sodium vegetable broth
- Fresh ground black pepper to taste

1. Take a large frying pan, heat oil over medium-high heat and fry onion and bell peppers for about four to five minutes.
2. Add garlic and fry for about a minute.
3. Add the remaining ingredients and stir to combine well.
4. Reduce the heat to medium and cook for about three to four minutes, stirring occasionally.
5. Serve hot.

Per Serving

Calories: **103** | Fat: **5.1g** | Sat Fat: **0.3g** | Carbs: **14.3g** | Fiber: **2.6g** | Sugar: **8.8g** | Protein: **2.1g**

CHEESY KALE CHIPS

Prep time: 10 minutes | Cook time: 15 minutes | Serves 4

- 4 tablespoons unsalted tahini
- 4 heaping tablespoons nutritional yeast
- ½ teaspoon garlic powder
- ½ cup water
- 1 large bunch of kale, cut into 2-inch chunks (about 5 tightly packed cups)

1. Preheat the oven to 400°F. Line a baking sheet with parchment paper.
2. In a large mixing bowl, combine the tahini, nutritional yeast, garlic powder, and water. The consistency should be runny enough to spread evenly over the kale.
3. Add the kale to the tahini mixture, thinly coating each kale piece, avoiding any clumpy chunks of sauce. Transfer the dipped kale to the prepared baking sheet and spread so that the pieces don't touch.
4. Bake for 10 to 15 minutes, until the edges become slightly browned and the kale turns into a crispy chip. Serve alongside your favorite main dish or enjoy as a crunchy snack. Store in a large container for up to 3 days; the crispiness starts to fade in 24 hours.

Per Serving

Calories: **130** | Total fat: **9g** | Saturated fat: **1g** | Carbs: **8g** | Sugars: **1g** | Fiber: **5g** | Protein: **8g**

FALL-SPICED APPLESAUCE

Prep time: **20 minutes** | Cook time: **4 hours on high or 8 hours on low** | Serves **8**

- 5 pounds apples (about 10 large), peeled, cored, and quartered
- juice of 1 lemon
- 2 teaspoons ground cinnamon
- ½ teaspoon ground nutmeg
- ¼ teaspoon ground cloves
- ¼ teaspoon ground ginger

1. Combine all the ingredients in a 4- or 6-quart slow cooker. Cover and cook on high for 4 hours or low for 8 hours.
2. Mash contents to your desired consistency using a potato masher or a slotted spoon.
3. Serve warm, or refrigerate for up to 5 days.

Per Serving

Calories: **140** | Total Fat: **0g** | Saturated Fat: **0g** |Sodium: **0mg** | Carbs: **38g** | Fiber: **4g** | Sugars: **29g** | Protein: **1g**

BUTTERNUT SQUASH FRIES

Prep time: **10 minutes** | Cook time: **15 minutes** | Serves **4**

- 1 medium butternut squash
- 1 tablespoon olive oil
- 1 tablespoon fresh thyme, chopped
- 1 tablespoon fresh rosemary, chopped
- ½ teaspoon salt

1. Preheat the oven to 425°F.
2. Grease a baking sheet with cooking spray.
3. Peel the squash and slice it into 3-inch-long and ½-inch wide pieces.
4. Place the pieces in a large bowl and toss with the oil, thyme, salt, and rosemary.
5. Spread the squash on the baking sheet and bake for 10 minutes.
6. Toss the fries well and bake again for 5 minutes or more until golden brown.
7. Serve.

Per Serving

Calories: **117** | Fat: **19g** |Sodium **57mg** | Carbs: **29g** | Fiber: **1.8g** | Sugar: **1.2g** | Protein: **2.5g**

VANILLA PEAR CRISP

Prep time: 10 minutes | Cook time: 4 to 5 hours on low | Serves 6

- 5 pears, chopped (peeling is optional)
- 1 apple, chopped (peeling is optional)
- ½ cup finely chopped dried figs
- ⅓ cup loosely packed brown sugar
- 2 teaspoons ground cinnamon
- 2 teaspoons vanilla extract
- 1 teaspoon ground nutmeg
- ½ cup whole-wheat flour, divided
- 1 cup old-fashioned oats
- ¼ cup honey
- 2 tablespoons coconut oil

1. Put the pears, apple, and figs in a 6-quart slow cooker.
2. In a small bowl, combine the brown sugar, cinnamon, vanilla, nutmeg, and ¼ cup of flour. Pour this over the fruit and stir to combine.
3. In the same small bowl, combine the oats, remaining ¼ cup of flour, honey, and coconut oil. Spread this mixture on top of the fruit.
4. Cover and cook on low for 4 to 5 hours, until the fruit is soft.
5. Serve warm.

Per Serving

Calories: **305** | Total Fat: **6g** | Saturated Fat: **4g** |Carbs: **64g** | Fiber: **8g** | Sugars: **39g** | Protein: **4g**

CASHEW AND CARDAMOM COOKIES

Prep time: 10 minutes | Cook time: 30 minutes | Serves 4

- Cooking spray
- 1 ½ cups all-purpose flour
- 2 tablespoons confectioners' sugar and ⅓ cup confectioners' sugar, divided use
- ½ cup light tub margarine
- 1 cup finely chopped cashews, dry-roasted
- 3 tablespoons cold water (as needed)
- 1 teaspoon ground cardamom
- 1 teaspoon vanilla extract

1. Preheat the oven to 350°F. Lightly spray a large baking sheet with cooking spray.
2. In a large bowl, sift together the flour and 2 tablespoons sugar. Using a fork or pastry blender, cut in the margarine. Stir in the cashews, up to 3 tablespoons water, the cardamom, and vanilla. Stir until the batter is just moistened but no flour is visible. Don't overmix.
3. Shape the batter into 24 small rolls, about 1 inch long and ½ inch thick. Transfer the rolls to the baking sheet, placing them 2 inches apart. Bake for 25 to 30 minutes, or until firm.
4. Meanwhile, spread the remaining ⅓ cup sugar on a separate large baking sheet. While the cookies are still warm, roll them in the sugar.

Per Serving

Calories: **84** | Total Fat: **4.0 g** | Saturated Fat: **0.5 g** |Carbs: **10 gg** | Fiber: **0 g** | Sugars: **3 g** | Protein: **2 g**

MACERATED STRAWBERRIES WITH HOMEMADE WHIPPED CREAM

Prep time: **5 minutes** | Cook time: **none**| Serves 6

- 2 cups sliced strawberries
- 2 tablespoons balsamic vinegar
- 3 tablespoons brown sugar
- ¼ teaspoon cracked black pepper

Whipped Cream

- ¼ cup cold heavy whipping cream
- ½ teaspoon vanilla extract
- 2 tablespoons brown sugar
- 1 ½ teaspoons grated orange zest

1. Place the strawberry slices in a large bowl. Add the vinegar and sugar, mix together, and let sit for at least 30 minutes so that the flavors meld and a syrupy sauce forms.
2. In a separate large bowl, whip the cold cream and vanilla with a hand mixer at high speed until bubbles form and the cream starts thickening. Add the sugar gradually while mixing and continue mixing until stiff peaks form. Fold in the orange zest with a spatula.
3. Dish the strawberries into small bowls, and top with black pepper and whipped cream. Drizzle some of the syrup from the strawberry bowl over the top.

Per Serving

Calories:**82** | Total Fat:**4 g** | Saturated Fat:**2 g** | Total Carbs:**15 g** | Fiber:**1 g** | Sugars:**13 g** | Protein:**0.5 g**

SOUR CREAM GREEN BEANS

Prep time: **10 minutes** | Cook time: **4 hours** | Serves **8**

- 15 ounces green beans
- 14 ounces corn
- 4 ounces mushrooms, sliced
- 11 ounces cream of mushroom soup, low-fat and sodium-free
- ½ cup low-fat sour cream
- ½ cup almonds, chopped
- ½ cup low-fat Cheddar cheese, shredded

1. In your slow cooker, mix the green beans with the corn, mushrooms soup, mushrooms, almonds, cheese and sour cream, toss
2. cover and cook on low for 4 hours.
3. Stir one more time, divide between plates and serve as a side dish.

Per Serving

Calories: **360** | Fat: **12.7g** | Sodium: **220mg** | Carbs: **58.3g** | Fiber: **10g** | Sugar: **10.3g** | Protein: **14g**

MAPLE-PECAN BRUSSELS SPROUTS

Prep time: **10 minutes** | Cook time: **4 to 5 hours on low** | Serves **6**

- 2 pounds brussels sprouts, halved (about 6 cups)
- 2 red onions, sliced
- ¼ cup pure maple syrup
- 2 tablespoons apple cider vinegar
- 1 tablespoon extra-virgin olive oil
- 1 teaspoon ground cinnamon
- ½ cup chopped pecans

1. Put the Brussels sprouts and onions in a 6-quart slow cooker.
2. In a small bowl, stir together the maple syrup, vinegar, cinnamon, and olive oil. Pour this mixture over the vegetables and toss to coat. Cover and cook on low for 4 to 5 hours. The Brussels sprouts should be softened but not mushy.
3. Add the pecans and stir to combine.

Per Serving

Calories: **176** | Total Fat: **10g** | Saturated Fat: **1g** | Carbs: **21g** | Fiber: **5g** | Sugars: **12g** | Protein: **4g**

STOVETOP APPLE CRISP

Prep time: **15 minutes** | Cook time: **20 minutes** | Serves **4**

- 1 pound red apples, cored and sliced (about 5)
- ⅓ cup water
- 1 teaspoon plus 1 tablespoon packed brown sugar, divided
- ¼ teaspoon freshly squeezed lemon juice (optional)
- ¼ cup rolled oats
- ¼ cup chopped walnuts
- 1 tablespoon unsalted butter
- ¼ teaspoon ground cinnamon
- pinch salt
- 2 tablespoons dried cranberries (optional)

1. Put the apples and water in a large pot or sauté pan, and bring to a boil over medium-high heat. When the water starts to boil, turn the heat down to medium-low, cover, and cook for 5 to 10 minutes. Check it and stir every few minutes, adding more water if needed.
2. When the apples are just about soft enough for your liking, take the lid off and cook until any excess liquid has evaporated. Taste an apple; add 1 teaspoon of brown sugar if they're too tart, or add the lemon juice if they're too sweet. (The cooking time and additions needed will vary by type of apple and personal preference.)
3. Meanwhile, combine the oats, walnuts, butter, cinnamon, salt, and 1 tablespoon of brown sugar in a small skillet. Cook over medium heat, stirring occasionally, until everything is toasty and fragrant.
4. Top the stewed apples with the crispy nuts and oats, as well as a sprinkle of dried cranberries, if you like.

Per Serving

Calories: **185** | Total Fat: **8g** | Saturated Fat: **2g** | Carbs: **29g** | Fiber: **4g** | Protein: **2g**

CHAPTER 6: SOUP & SALAD SYMPHONY

LENTIL AND FENNEL SALAD

Prep time: 10 minutes | Cook time: 20 minutes | Serves 4

- 1 cup dried brown or green lentils
- 2 carrots, grated
- 1 fennel bulb, cored and thinly sliced
- ½ cup chopped fresh parsley
- ½ cup Lemon Vinaigrette

1. In a large saucepan, cover the lentils with water by a few inches. Bring to a boil over high heat.
2. Reduce the heat to medium. Simmer for 15 to 20 minutes, or until the lentils are tender but not mushy. Remove from the heat. Drain, and rinse with cold water to cool.
3. While the lentils are cooking, in a large bowl, toss together the carrots, fennel, parsley, and vinaigrette. Let sit until the lentils are ready.
4. Add the lentils, and gently mix.

Per Serving

Calories: 372 | Total fat: 19g | Saturated fat: 2g | Sodium: 284mg | Carbs: 41g | Fiber: 8g | Protein: 13g | Calcium: 72mg

MIDDLE EASTERN LAMB STEW

Prep time: 10 minutes | Cook time: 7 to 8 hours on low | Serves 8

- 2 pounds boneless lamb stew meat, cut into 1-inch chunks, or 2½ pounds lamb shoulder chops, deboned and trimmed
- 1 (28-ounce) can no-salt-added diced tomatoes
- 1 (14.5-ounce) can chickpeas, drained and rinsed
- ¾ cup beef stock or low-sodium beef broth
- 1 large onion, chopped
- 2 garlic cloves, minced
- 2 teaspoons grated fresh ginger
- 2 teaspoons ground cumin
- ½ teaspoon ground cinnamon
- ½ teaspoon dried mint
- ¼ teaspoon freshly ground black pepper
- 1 tablespoon freshly squeezed lemon juice
- pinch salt

1. Place the lamb in a 6-quart slow cooker. Add the tomatoes, chickpeas, stock, onion, garlic, ginger, cumin, cinnamon, mint, and pepper and stir well. Cover and cook on low for 7 to 8 hours.
2. Turn off the slow cooker and stir in the lemon juice and salt. Let the stew stand for 5 minutes to allow the flavors to blend. Serve warm.

Per Serving

Calories: 251 | Total Fat: 9g | Saturated Fat: 4g | Carbs: 18g | Fiber: 4g | Sugars: 6g | Protein: 27g

ZESTY LIME SHRIMP AND AVOCADO SALAD

Prep time: 10 minutes | Cook time: none | Serves 4

- ¼ cup chopped red onion
- Juice of 1 lime
- 1 teaspoon olive oil
- ⅛ teaspoon salt
- ⅛ teaspoon freshly ground black pepper
- ½ pound cooked, peeled, and chopped jumbo shrimp
- 1 medium tomato, diced
- ½ large avocado, diced
- 1 tablespoon chopped fresh cilantro
- 1 tablespoon chopped fresh oregano
- 4 cups romaine leaves, chopped

1. In a small bowl, combine the red onion, lime juice, olive oil, salt, and pepper. Let it marinate for at least 5 minutes for the flavors to combine.
2. In a large bowl, combine the shrimp, tomato, and avocado and toss gently. Add the cilantro and oregano and toss gently again.
3. Divide the romaine lettuce between two serving bowls and spoon half of the shrimp mixture over the top of each mound and drizzle with half of the dressing. Serve immediately.

Per Serving

Calories: 283 | Fats: 15g | Protein: 28g | Cholesterol: 239mg | Carbs: 12g | Fiber: 5g | Sodium: 433mg

PEAR AND PUMPKIN SEED SALAD

Prep time: 20 minutes | Cook time: 20 minutes | Serves 4

For The Dressing:

- 3 tablespoons extra-virgin olive oil
- 2 teaspoons dijon mustard
- 2 teaspoons cooking sherry
- 2 teaspoons red wine vinegar

For The Salad:

- 1 head butter lettuce, torn into pieces
- 2 bosc pears, cored and cut into bite-size pieces
- ¼ cup salted shelled pumpkin seeds
- ½ cup grated parmesan cheese
- freshly ground black pepper (optional)

1. In a large bowl, whisk together the oil, mustard, sherry, and vinegar.
2. Add the lettuce and pears, and toss well to coat with the dressing.
3. Top with the pumpkin seeds, Parmesan cheese, and a grind of pepper, if you like.

Per Serving

Calories: 244 | Total Fat: 17g | Saturated Fat: 4g | Carbs: 18g | Fiber: 4g | Protein: 7g

CANNELLINI BEAN AND SWISS CHARD SOUP

Prep time: **15 minutes** | Cook time: **45 minutes** | Serves **4**

- 2 teaspoons avocado oil
- ½ cup shallots, diced
- 1 bunch of swiss chard, divided (1 cup stems, diced into bite-size pieces and 6 cups leaves, chopped)
- 2 medium parsnips, cut into bite-size pieces (about 1 cup)
- 1 cup water
- 3 cups no-salt-added cannellini beans
- 4 cups low-sodium vegetable broth or homemade vegetable broth
- ¼ teaspoon freshly ground black pepper

1. In a 5-quart pot, heat the oil over medium heat. Add the shallots, Swiss chard stems, and parsnips and cook for about 5 minutes, until the shallots are translucent and the parsnips are lightly browned.
2. Add in the Swiss chard leaves, water, beans, broth, and pepper and mix well. Cook for 40 minutes, covered, stirring occasionally. Serve or store in the refrigerator for 3 to 4 days, or freeze in an airtight container for up to 4 months.

Per Serving

Calories: **284** | Total fat: **4g** | Carbs: **44g** | Sugars: **6g** | Fiber: **14g** | Protein: **12g**

ROOT VEGETABLE STEW

Prep time: **15 minutes** | Cook time: **6 to 8 hours on low** | Serves **6 to 8**

- 1 pound yukon gold potatoes, diced
- 1 pound sweet potatoes, diced
- 1 pound parsnips, diced
- 1 pound carrots, diced
- 4 cups savory vegetable broth
- 3 cups diced butternut squash
- 2 medium beets, peeled and diced
- 2 medium onions, diced
- 1 (15-ounce) can chickpeas, drained and rinsed
- 4 garlic cloves, minced
- 2 bay leaves
- 2 teaspoons dried sage
- freshly ground black pepper

1. Combine all the ingredients in a 6-quart slow cooker. Cover and cook on low for 6 to 8 hours, until the vegetables are tender.
2. Remove and discard the bay leaves and serve hot.

Per Serving

Calories: **357** | Total Fat: **0g** | Saturated Fat: **0g** | Carbs: **81g** | Fiber: **16g** | Sugars: **30g** | Protein: **10g**

ROASTED SUMMER SQUASH FARRO SALAD

Prep time: 10 minutes | Cook time: 20 minutes | Serves 2

- 1 cup water
- ¼ cup farro
- 1 medium yellow squash, cut into ½-inch-thick pieces
- 1 medium green zucchini, cut into ½-inch-thick pieces
- 1 teaspoon dried basil
- ½ teaspoon freshly ground black pepper
- 2 tablespoons Arugula-Basil Pesto

1. Preheat the oven to 450°F. Line a baking sheet with parchment paper.
2. In a small saucepan, bring the water to a boil and add the farro. Reduce the heat, cover, and bring to a simmer for 20 minutes. Once the water has soaked into the farro, fluff it with a fork.
3. In the meantime, place the squash, zucchini, basil, and pepper on the baking sheet and coat with the spice mixture. Bake for 10 minutes, then flip and stir the pieces and bake for an additional 5 minutes.
4. In a medium mixing bowl, combine the farro, vegetables, and pesto. Serve immediately or chilled. The salad can be stored in an airtight container in the refrigerator for up to 4 days.

Per Serving

Calories: 225 | Total fat: 11g | Saturated fat: 1g | Carbs: 28g | Sugars: 5g | Fiber: 7g | Protein: 7g

TEX-MEX CUCUMBER SALAD

Prep time: 10 minutes | Cook time: 5 minutes | Serves 4

- 1 medium cucumber, peeled, seeded, and diced
- 1 medium tomato, seeded and diced
- ⅓ cup picante sauce (lowest sodium available)
- 2 medium green onions, finely chopped
- 2 tablespoons chopped fresh cilantro
- 1 tablespoon fresh lime juice
- 1 tablespoon olive oil (extra-virgin preferred)
- 1 medium garlic clove, minced

1. In a small bowl, stir together all the ingredients.
2. Serve immediately for peak flavor.

Per Serving

Calories: 55 | Total Fat: 3.5 g | Saturated Fat: 0.5 g |Carbs: 5 gg | Fiber: 1 g | Sugars: 3 g | Protein: 1 g

CANNERY ROW SOUP

Prep time: **15 minutes** | Cook time: **15 minutes** | Serves **8**

- 2 tbsp olive oil
- 3 carrots, cut in thin strips
- 2 cups celery, sliced
- ½ cup onion, chopped
- ¼ cup green peppers, chopped
- 1 clove garlic, minced
- 1 can (28 oz) whole tomatoes, cut up, with liquid
- 1 cup clam juice
- ¼ tsp dried thyme, crushed
- ¼ tsp dried basil, crushed
- ⅛ tsp black pepper
- 2 lb varied fish fillets, cut into 1-inch cubes
- ¼ cup fresh parsley, minced

1. Heat oil in large saucepan. Sauté garlic, carrots, celery, onion, and green pepper in oil for 3 minutes.
2. Add remaining ingredients, except for parsley and fish. Cover and simmer for 10 to 15 minutes or until vegetables are fork tender.
3. Add fish and parsley. Simmer covered for 5 to 10 minutes more or until fish flakes easily and is opaque. Serve hot.

Per Serving:

Calories: **170**| Total Fat:**5g**| Saturated Fat: **1g**| Cholesterol: **56mg**| Sodium: **380mg**| Total Fiber: **3g**| Protein: **22g**| Carbs: **9g**

CLASSIC CAPRESE SALAD

Prep time: **15 minutes** | Cook time: **15 minutes** | Serves **4**

- 6 small tomatoes
- 8 ounces fresh mozzarella cheese
- ¼ teaspoon kosher salt, plus more if needed
- freshly ground black pepper (optional)
- ⅓ cup torn fresh basil leaves
- 2 tablespoons extra-virgin olive oil
- 2 tablespoons balsamic vinegar

1. Use a serrated knife to cut the tomatoes and cheese into ¼-inch slices. You should have about the same number of each. If not, cut some pieces in half. so you do
2. Arrange the tomatoes and cheese on a serving platter in alternating slices.
3. Sprinkle with salt and pepper (if using). Spread the basil over the salad. Drizzle with the olive oil and balsamic vinegar. Taste and adjust the seasoning.

Per Serving

Calories: **252** | Total Fat: **21g** | Saturated Fat: **9g** | Carbs: **7g** | Fiber: **2g** | Protein: **11g**

CHAPTER 7: OCEAN'S BOUNTY

SESAME-CRUSTED TUNA STEAKS

Prep time: **5 minutes** | Cook time: **12 minutes** | Serves **4**

- Olive oil nonstick cooking spray
- ½ tablespoon olive oil
- 1 teaspoon sesame oil
- 2 (6-ounce) ahi tuna steaks
- 6 tablespoons sesame seeds
- Salt
- Freshly ground black pepper

1. Preheat the oven to 450°F and lightly spray a baking sheet with cooking spray.
2. In a small bowl, stir together the olive oil and sesame oil. Brush the tuna steaks with the oil mixture.
3. Put the sesame seeds in a shallow bowl. Press the steaks into the seeds, turning to cover all sides.
4. Place the tuna steaks on the prepared baking sheet. Sprinkle with salt and pepper. Bake for 4 to 6 minutes per ½-inch thickness of fish, or until the fish begins to flake when tested with a fork. Serve immediately.

Per Serving

Calories: **520** | Fats: **30g** | Protein: **56g** | Cholesterol: **83mg** | Carbs: **6g** | Fiber: **3g** | Sodium: **166mg**

ITALIAN-STYLE TUNA SALAD

Prep time: **5 minutes** | Cook time: **none** | Serves **4**

- 2 (5-ounce) cans albacore tuna in water, no salt added, drained
- ½ cup chopped Roma tomato
- ¼ cup chopped red onion
- 4 tablespoons finely chopped fresh parsley
- Juice of 1 lemon
- 4 tablespoons extra virgin olive oil
- ⅛ teaspoon cracked black pepper

1. Place all the ingredients in a large bowl, and stir to incorporate evenly.
2. Let sit for 30 minutes before serving.

Per Serving

Calories:**205** | Total Fat:**15 g** | Saturated Fat:**2 g** | Total Carbs:**4 g** | Fiber:**2 g** | Sugars:**0 g** | Protein:**19 g**

SEAFOOD STEW

Prep time: 10 minutes | Cook time: 30 minutes | Serves 4

- ½ medium yellow onion, chopped
- ½ Jalapeno pepper, chopped
- ½ pound red snapper fillets, cubed
- ¼ pound fresh tomatoes, chopped
- ⅛ pound fresh squid, cleaned and cut into rings
- ⅛ pound mussels
- ¼ cup fresh parsley, chopped
- 1 tablespoon olive oil
- 3/2 garlic cloves, minced
- ⅛ teaspoon red pepper flakes, crushed
- ¾ cup low-sodium fish broth
- ¼ pound shrimp, peeled and deveined
- ⅛ pound bay scallops
- 1 tablespoon fresh lemon juice

1. Take a large soup pan, heat oil over medium heat and fry the onion for about five to six minutes.
2. Add the garlic, Serrano pepper and red pepper flakes and fry for another minute.
3. Include tomatoes and broth and bring to a gentle simmer.
4. Reduce the heat to low and cook for about ten minutes.
5. Add the snapper and cook for about two minutes.
6. Stir in the remaining seafood and cook for about six to eight minutes.
7. Stir in the lemon juice, basil, salt and black pepper and remove from heat.
8. Serve hot and enjoy!

Per Serving

Calories: 1024 | Fat: 18.6g | Sat Fat: 4.4g | Carbs: 33g | Fiber: 1.1g | Sugar: 1.7g | Protein: 168.7g

SALMON BURGERS WITH DILL

Prep time: **5 minutes** | Cook time: **35 minutes** | Serves **4**

- 1 pound salmon fillets
- ½ teaspoon salt, divided
- ¼ teaspoon freshly ground black pepper
- ½ cup bread crumbs
- 1 large egg
- 2 garlic cloves, minced
- ½ teaspoon dried dill
- 2 tablespoons extra-virgin olive oil

1. Preheat the oven to 400°F. Line a baking sheet with parchment paper.
2. Put the salmon on the prepared baking sheet. Season with ¼ teaspoon of salt and the pepper.
3. Transfer the baking sheet to the oven, and bake for 15 to 20 minutes, or until the salmon flakes with a fork. Remove from the oven.
4. Remove the salmon flesh from the skin. Transfer the flesh to a bowl, removing any bones.
5. Mix in the bread crumbs, egg, garlic, dill, and remaining ¼ teaspoon of salt.
6. Form the mixture into 4 patties.
7. In a large skillet, heat the oil over medium heat.
8. Add the patties, and cook for 5 to 6 minutes, or until browned. Flip, and cook on the other side for 3 to 5 minutes. Remove from the heat.

Per Serving

Calories: **294** | Total fat: **16g** | Saturated fat: **3g** | Sodium: **458mg** | Carbs: **10g** | Fiber: **1g** | Protein: **26g**

OVEN-FRIED SCALLOPS WITH CILANTRO AND LIME

Prep time: **10 minutes** | Cook time: **13 minutes** | Serves **4**

- Cooking spray
- ½ cup low-fat buttermilk
- 2 tablespoons chopped fresh cilantro and 2 tablespoons chopped fresh cilantro, divided use
- 2 tablespoons fresh lime juice
- ¼ teaspoon pepper
- 1 pound sea scallops, rinsed and patted dry
- ½ cup whole-wheat panko (Japanese-style bread crumbs)
- Dash of paprika
- 1 medium lime, cut into 4 wedges (optional)

1. Preheat the oven to 400°F. Lightly spray a 9-inch round or square baking pan with cooking spray.
2. In a shallow glass bowl, whisk together the buttermilk, 2 tablespoons cilantro, lime juice, and pepper.
3. Stir the scallops into the buttermilk mixture, turning to coat. Let soak for 10 minutes. Drain, discarding the buttermilk mixture.
4. Put the panko on a plate. Roll the scallops in the panko to coat, gently shaking off any excess. Arrange the scallops in a single layer in the baking pan.
5. Sprinkle the paprika over the scallops. Lightly spray with cooking spray.
6. Bake for 10 to 13 minutes, or until opaque. Be careful not to overcook or the scallops will become rubbery. Just before serving, sprinkle with the remaining 2 tablespoons cilantro. Serve with the lime wedges.

Per Serving

Calories: **132** | Total Fat: **1.0 g** | Saturated Fat: **0.0 g** | Carbs: **9 gg** | Fiber: **0 g** | Sugars: **1 g** | Protein: **20 g**

SPICY SHRIMP, FETA, AND WALNUT COUSCOUS

Prep time: **25 minutes** | Cook time: **30 minutes** | Serves **4**

- 1 tablespoon extra-virgin olive oil
- 2 cups frozen sliced onions and bell peppers
- 2 medium ripe tomatoes, chopped
- 2 garlic cloves, minced
- 1½ cups reduced-sodium chicken broth
- ½ teaspoon cayenne pepper
- 12 ounces sustainably sourced, frozen raw shrimp, thawed and peeled
- 1 cup uncooked whole-wheat couscous
- ⅓ cup chopped walnuts
- ⅓ cup crumbled feta cheese

1. Heat the oil in a large, heavy skillet over medium-high heat. When the oil is hot, add the onions and peppers. Cook, stirring occasionally, for 3 to 4 minutes.
2. Add the tomato and garlic, and cook for 1 minute. Add the chicken broth and cayenne pepper, and bring to a boil. Add the shrimp, and return to a boil.
3. Stir in the couscous. Remove the skillet from the heat, cover, and let stand until the couscous is tender and all the broth is absorbed, about 5 minutes.
4. Fluff with a fork. Top with the walnuts and feta cheese.

Per Serving

Calories: **392** | Total Fat: **14g** | Saturated Fat: **3g** | Carbs: **40g** | Fiber: **5g** | Added Sugars: **g** | Protein: **29g**

BAKED SALMON DIJON

Prep time: 5 minutes | **Cook time: 20 minutes** | **Serves 6**

- 1 cup fat-free sour cream
- 3 tbsp scallions, finely chopped
- 2 tbsp dijon mustard
- 2 tbsp lemon juice
- 2 tsp dried dill
- 1½ lb salmon fillet with skin, cut in center
- ½ tsp garlic powder
- ½ tsp black pepper
- as needed fat-free cooking spray

1. Whisk sour cream, scallions, mustard, lemon juice, and dill in small bowl to blend.
2. Preheat oven to 400°F. Lightly oil baking sheet with cooking spray.
3. Place salmon, skin side down, on prepared sheet. Sprinkle with garlic powder and pepper, then spread the sauce.
4. Bake salmon until just opaque in center, about 20 minutes.

Per Serving

Calories: **196** | Total Fat: **7g** | Saturated Fat: **2g** | Cholesterol: **76mg** | Sodium: **229mg** | Total Fiber: **1g** | Protein: **27g** | Carbs: **5g**

CHAPTER 8: POULTRY PALATE

CHICKEN WITH ORANGE SAUCE

Prep time: 10 minutes | **Cook time: 57 minutes** | **Serves 4**

- Cooking spray
- ½ teaspoon paprika
- 1 2 ½-pound chicken, skin and all visible fat discarded, cut into serving pieces
- 1 medium onion, sliced

Sauce

- ½ cup 100% frozen orange juice concentrate
- ⅓ cup water
- 2 tablespoons light brown sugar
- 2 tablespoons chopped fresh parsley
- 1 teaspoon soy sauce (lowest sodium available)
- 1 teaspoon dry sherry (optional)
- ½ teaspoon ground ginger

1. Preheat the broiler. Lightly spray a heavy-duty baking sheet with cooking spray.
2. Sprinkle the paprika over the chicken. Put the chicken on the baking sheet.
3. Broil the chicken about 6 inches from the heat for about 2 minutes on each side, or until lightly browned. Transfer the chicken to a Dutch oven or large deep skillet.
4. Spread the onion over the chicken.
5. In a small bowl, whisk together the sauce ingredients. Pour over the chicken and onion.
6. Bring to a boil over medium-high heat. Reduce the heat and simmer, covered, for 55 minutes to 1 hour, or until the chicken is no longer pink in the center.

Per Serving

Calories: **272** | Total Fat: **7.0 g** | Saturated Fat: **2.0 g** | Carbs: **24 gg** | Fiber: **1 g** | Sugars: **22 g** | Protein: **28 g**

ROASTED TOMATO AND CHICKEN PASTA

Prep time: 20 minutes | **Cook time: 30 minutes** | **Serves 4**

- 1 pound boneless, skinless chicken thighs, cut into bite-size pieces
- ⅛ teaspoon kosher salt (optional)
- ¼ teaspoon freshly ground black pepper (optional)
- 4 cups cherry tomatoes, halved
- 4 garlic cloves, minced
- 1 tablespoon canola or sunflower oil
- 1 teaspoon dried basil
- 8 ounces uncooked whole-wheat rotini
- 10 kalamata olives, pitted and sliced
- ¼ teaspoon red pepper flakes (optional)
- ¼ cup grated parmesan cheese (optional)

1. Preheat the oven to 450°F.
2. Season the chicken with salt and pepper, if desired. Toss the chicken in a large bowl with the tomatoes, garlic, oil, and basil. Transfer to a rimmed baking sheet, and spread out evenly.
3. Roast until the chicken is cooked through, 15 to 20 minutes, tossing halfway though. A meat thermometer should read 165°F.
4. Meanwhile, cook the pasta to al dente according to the package directions. Drain.
5. In a large serving bowl, toss the chicken and tomatoes with the pasta, olives, and pepper flakes (if using). Top with Parmesan, if desired.

Per Serving

Calories: **458** | Total Fat: **14g** | Carbs: **52g** | Fiber: **8g** | Added Sugars: **0g** | Protein: **34g**

SHREDDED CHICKEN SLOPPY JOES

Prep time: **15 minutes** | Cook time: **6 to 7 hours on low** | Serves **8**

- 2 pounds boneless, skinless chicken breasts
- 1 (14-ounce) can tomato sauce
- 1 cup finely shredded carrots
- 4 dates, pitted and finely chopped
- ¼ cup tomato paste
- 1 jalapeño pepper, seeded and diced
- 4 garlic cloves, minced
- 3 tablespoons yellow mustard
- 2 tablespoons apple cider vinegar
- 1 teaspoon chili powder
- 1 teaspoon onion powder
- freshly ground black pepper

1. Combine all the ingredients in a 6-quart slow cooker. Cover and cook on low for 6 to 7 hours.
2. Remove the chicken from the slow cooker and shred it with two forks. Return the chicken to the slow cooker, stir to mix, and continue cooking until ready to serve.
3. Serve hot.

Per Serving

Calories: **182** | Total Fat: **4g** | Carbs: **9g** | Fiber: **2g** | Sugars: **6g** | Protein: **28g**

CHICKEN LETTUCE WRAP WITH PEANUT DRESSING

Prep time: **10 minutes** | Cook time: **5 minutes** | Serves **2**

- 2 teaspoons avocado oil
- 2 garlic cloves, minced, divided
- ½ cup diced shallots
- 8 ounces lean ground chicken or turkey breast
- 1 teaspoon grated ginger
- 3 tablespoons unsalted peanut butter
- 4 tablespoons water
- 6 large butter lettuce leaves

1. In a medium skillet, heat the oil over medium heat. Add 1 minced garlic clove and the shallots and cook for 1 to 2 minutes, until sizzling and translucent.
2. Add the ground chicken and break into pieces. Stir the ground meat until lightly golden and cooked through, about 5 minutes.
3. In a small mixing bowl, combine the ginger, remaining garlic clove, peanut butter, and water. Add to the chicken mixture on the stovetop. Cook for about 1 minute until all flavors have combined.
4. Divide the chicken mixture into the lettuce cups and serve. Alternatively, this dish can be stored in an airtight container in the refrigerator for up to 3 days.

Per Serving

Calories: **414** | Total fat: **21g** | Saturated fat: **4g** | Carbs: **17g** | Sugars: **7g** | Fiber: **4g** | Protein: **32g**

PAN-SEARED CHICKEN

Prep time: **10 minutes** | Cook time: **20 minutes** | Serves **4**

- 1 pound boneless, skinless chicken breasts
- ¼ teaspoon kosher salt
- freshly ground black pepper
- 2 tablespoons canola or sunflower oil

1. Pat the chicken dry with paper towels. Season with the salt and pepper.
2. Heat a large, heavy skillet over medium-high heat. Add the canola or sunflower oil. When the oil is hot (a drop of water should sizzle), add the chicken—make sure there is oil under each piece. Cover the pan.
3. After 5 minutes, check that the undersides are crispy and golden, and flip them over. If they feel stuck, give them another minute or two.
4. Cover and cook the other side for 5 minutes more, without disturbing the chicken. Use a meat thermometer to ensure that it has reached 165°F inside. It should be opaque with mostly clear juices. Transfer the chicken to a cutting board. Let it rest for a few minutes before slicing.

Per Serving

Calories: **198** | Total Fat: **10g** | Saturated Fat: **1g** | Carbs: **0g** | Fiber: **0g** | **Added** Sugars: **0g** | Protein: **26g**

SPICY GRILLED CHICKEN

Prep time: **10 minutes** | Cook time: **7 minutes** | Serves **4**

- 1 small red onion, finely chopped
- 3 tablespoons fresh lime juice (about 2 medium limes)
- 2 tablespoons olive oil
- 2 tablespoons finely chopped fresh cilantro
- ½ teaspoon chili powder
- ½ teaspoon ground cumin
- ¼ teaspoon salt
- 1 small garlic clove, minced
- ½ medium fresh jalapeño, seeds and ribs discarded, minced
- 8 boneless, skinless chicken breast halves (about 4 ounces each), all visible fat discarded
- Cooking spray

1. In a large shallow glass dish, whisk together the marinade ingredients. Add the chicken, turning to coat. Cover and refrigerate for 2 to 3 hours, turning occasionally.
2. Lightly spray the grill rack with cooking spray. Preheat the grill on medium high.
3. Grill the chicken for 6 to 7 minutes on each side, or until no longer pink in the center.

Per Serving

Calories: **129** | Total Fat: **3.0 g** | Saturated Fat: **0.5 g** | Carbs: **0 gg** | Fiber: **0 g** | Sugars: **0 g** | Protein: **24 g**

TURKEY MEATBALLS

Prep time: 10 minutes | Cook time: 30 minutes | Serves 5

- Cooking spray
- 1 pound ground skinless turkey breast
- 1 small onion, grated
- ⅓ cup shredded or grated Parmesan cheese
- ¼ cup whole-wheat bread crumbs (lowest sodium available)
- 3 tablespoons chopped fresh parsley
- 1 large egg, well beaten
- 1 medium garlic clove, minced
- ¼ teaspoon ground nutmeg
- ¼ teaspoon pepper
- ¼ cup all-purpose flour

1. Preheat the oven to 350°F. Lightly spray the broiler pan and rack with cooking spray.
2. In a medium bowl, using your hands or a spoon, combine the meatball ingredients. Shape into 35 balls, about 1 inch in diameter. Dust with the flour. Transfer to the broiler rack.
3. Broil the meatballs about 4 inches from the heat for 10 to 15 minutes, or until the tops are browned. Turn over the meatballs. Broil for 10 to 15 minutes, or until the meatballs are browned on the outside and no longer pink in the center.

Per Serving

Calories: 190 | Total Fat: 4.0 g | Saturated Fat: 1.5 g | Carbs: 12 gg | Fiber: 1 g | Sugars: 2 g | Protein: 28 g

SESAME SOY CHICKEN

Prep time: 10 minutes | Cook time: 30 minutes | Serves 6

- 1 cup finely chopped onion
- 1 teaspoon grated lime zest
- ½ cup fresh lime juice (about 4 large limes)
- ⅓ cup sherry or fresh orange juice
- ¼ cup frozen 100% orange juice concentrate, thawed
- 3 tablespoons soy sauce (lowest sodium available)
- 2 tablespoons
- grated peeled gingerroot
- 1 tablespoon sugar
- 1 tablespoon hot chili oil
- 3 medium garlic cloves, minced
- 6 boneless, skinless chicken breast halves (about 4 ounces each), all visible fat discarded
- 1 tablespoon sesame seeds, dry-roasted

1. In a large broilerproof baking dish, stir together the onion, lime zest, lime juice, sherry, soy sauce, orange juice concentrate, gingerroot, sugar, hot chili oil, and garlic. Add the chicken, turning to coat. Cover and refrigerate for several hours or overnight, turning the chicken occasionally.
2. Preheat the oven to 400°F.
3. Bake the chicken with the marinade for 20 to 25 minutes, or until the chicken is no longer pink in the center. Remove from the oven. Preheat the broiler. Broil the chicken mixture for 5 minutes, turning the chicken halfway through. Just before serving, sprinkle with the sesame seeds.

Per Serving

Calories: 215 | Total Fat: 6.5 g | Saturated Fat: 1.0 g | Carbs: 13 gg | Fiber: 1 g | Sugars: 9 g | Protein: 26 g

CHAPTER 9: MEAT MEDLEY

YOGURT-MARINATED GRILLED ROUND STEAK

Prep time: **10 minutes** | Cook time: **13 minutes** | Serves **4**

Marinade

- 6 ounces fat-free plain yogurt
- ¼ cup thinly sliced green onions
- 2 tablespoons chopped fresh parsley (Italian, or flat-leaf, preferred)
- 2 teaspoons grated lemon zest
- 1 tablespoon fresh lemon juice
- 1 medium garlic clove, minced
- 1 1-pound boneless round steak, all visible fat discarded
- ¼ cup fat-free sour cream
- ¼ teaspoon salt

1. In a large shallow glass dish, stir together the marinade ingredients. Pour ¼ cup marinade into a small bowl. Add the beef to the remaining marinade, turning to coat. Cover and refrigerate the beef for 8 hours, turning occasionally.
2. Stir the sour cream into the marinade in the small bowl. Cover and refrigerate until ready to serve.
3. Preheat the grill on medium high.
4. Scrape the marinade off the beef, discarding the marinade. Sprinkle the salt over the beef.
5. Grill the beef for 6 to 8 minutes on each side, or to the desired doneness. Transfer to a cutting board and let stand for 3 to 5 minutes. Thinly slice the beef diagonally across the grain. Serve with the sauce.

Per Serving

Calories: **158** | Total Fat: **3.0 g** | Saturated Fat: **1.0 g** | Carbs: **4 gg** | Fiber: **0 g** | Sugars: **2 g** | Protein: **28 g**

BEEF PITA SANDWICHES

Prep time: **5 minutes** | Cook time: **15 minutes** | Serves **4**

- 12 ounces flank steak
- ½ teaspoon garlic powder
- ½ teaspoon salt
- ¼ teaspoon freshly ground black pepper
- 2 tablespoons extra-virgin olive oil
- 4 whole-wheat pita rounds, halved
- ½ cup Tahini Dressing

1. Season the steak with the garlic powder, salt, and pepper.
2. In a large skillet, heat the oil over medium-high heat.
3. Add the steak, and sear for 5 to 7 minutes per side, or until cooked to your desired doneness. Remove from the heat. Let rest for 5 minutes, then thinly slice against the grain.
4. Stuff several slices of steak into the pita halves.
5. Drizzle with the dressing.

Per Serving

Calories: **377** | Total fat: **23g** | Saturated fat: **4g** | Sodium: **714mg** | Carbs: **23g** | Fiber: **4g** | Protein: **25g**

LAMB ROAST WITH ROOT VEGETABLES

Prep time: 10 minutes | Cook time: 7 to 8 hours on low | Serves 8

- 4 pounds cubed lamb meat
- 4 garlic cloves, minced
- 2 or 3 fresh rosemary sprigs
- nonstick cooking spray
- 2 teaspoons freshly ground black pepper
- 6 carrots, sliced
- 4 beets, peeled and cut into wedges
- 2 medium parsnips, peeled and sliced
- 2 medium sweet potatoes, peeled and cut into wedges
- 2 medium turnips, peeled and cut into wedges
- 2 medium yukon gold potatoes, cut into wedges
- 2 cups chicken stock or low-sodium chicken broth

1. Make incisions in roast and press in the garlic and rosemary.
2. Lightly coat the bowl of a 6-quart slow cooker with the cooking spray. Place the lamb into the slow cooker and sprinkle it with the black pepper. Place any loose rosemary leaves in the slow cooker, too.
3. Arrange the carrots, beets, parsnips, sweet potatoes, turnips, and potatoes around the meat. Pour in the stock. Cover and cook on low for 7 to 8 hours, until the vegetables are tender and the meat reaches an internal temperature of 160°F.
4. Remove the roast and let rest for 5 to 10 minutes before slicing and serving.

Per Serving

Calories: **459** | Total Fat: **12g** | Saturated Fat: **4g** |Carbs: **34g** | Fiber: **6g** | Sugars: **11g** | Protein: **49g**

BEEF AND EGGPLANT CASSEROLE

Prep time: 10 minutes | Cook time: 55 minutes | Serves 4

- Cooking spray
- 1 pound extra-lean ground beef
- 1 ½ medium onions, chopped
- 1 ½ tablespoons dried dillweed, crumbled
- 2 medium garlic cloves, chopped
- Pepper to taste (freshly ground preferred)
- 1 medium eggplant or 3 medium yellow summer squash, or a combination, cut into vertical slices about ⅛ inch thick
- 2 cups fat-free plain yogurt

1. Preheat the oven to 350°F. Lightly spray an 8-inch square casserole dish with cooking spray.
2. In a medium skillet, cook the beef over medium-high heat for 8 to 10 minutes, or until browned on the outside and no longer pink in the center, stirring occasionally to turn and break up the beef. Stir in the onions, dillweed, garlic, and pepper.
3. Arrange some of the eggplant slices in a single layer in the casserole dish. Spoon a layer of the beef mixture over the eggplant. Repeat these layers. Top with a layer of eggplant. Spoon the yogurt over all.
4. Bake for 45 minutes to 1 hour, or until bubbly.

Per Serving

Calories: **274** | Total Fat: **6.0 g** | Saturated Fat: **2.5 g** | Carbs: **23 gg** | Fiber: **5 g** | Sugars: **17 g** | Protein: **33 g**

BEEF AND PASTA SKILLET

Prep time: **10 minutes** | Cook time: **15 minutes** | Serves **6**

- 8 ounces dried tricolor rotini
- 8 ounces extra-lean ground beef
- 8 ounces button mushrooms, sliced
- 1 large onion, chopped
- 3 medium garlic cloves, minced
- 1 ½ teaspoons dried Italian seasoning, crumbled
- 1 ½ teaspoons dried basil, crumbled
- 1 cup water
- 1 6-ounce can no-salt-added tomato paste
- 2 tablespoons shredded or grated Parmesan cheese
- 2 tablespoons finely chopped fresh parsley
- 1 teaspoon Worcestershire sauce (lowest sodium available)
- ¼ teaspoon salt

1. Prepare the pasta using the package directions, omitting the salt. Drain well in a colander.
2. Meanwhile, in a large skillet, stir together the beef, mushrooms, onion, garlic, Italian seasoning, and basil. Cook, covered, over medium-high heat for 8 to 10 minutes, or until the beef is no longer pink and the mushrooms have released their liquid and are fully cooked, stirring occasionally to turn and break up the beef.
3. In a small bowl, whisk together the remaining ingredients. Stir the tomato paste mixture and the pasta into the beef mixture. Cook for 5 minutes.

Per Serving

Calories: **246** | Total Fat: **3.0 g** | Saturated Fat: **1.0 g** | Carbs: **39 gg** | Fiber: **3 g** | Sugars: **8 g** | Protein: **17 g**

HERB-CRUSTED PORK TENDERLOIN

Prep time: **5 minutes** | Cook time: **30 minutes** | Serves **6**

- 1 teaspoon dried thyme
- ½ teaspoon ground cumin
- ½ teaspoon onion powder
- ¼ teaspoon salt
- ¼ teaspoon freshly
- ground black pepper
- 1½ pounds pork tenderloin
- 1 tablespoon extra-virgin olive oil
- 3 garlic cloves, minced

1. Preheat the oven to 400°F.
2. In a small bowl, combine the thyme, cumin, onion powder, salt, and pepper. Mix well.
3. Press the mixture into the pork tenderloin on all sides.
4. In an oven-safe skillet, heat the oil over medium-high heat.
5. Add the garlic, and cook for 30 seconds, or until fragrant.
6. Add the pork, and brown on all sides for 2 to 3 minutes per side. Turn off the heat.
7. Transfer the skillet to the oven, and cook for 15 to 20 minutes, depending on the thickness, or until the pork has cooked through. Remove from the oven.

Per Serving

Calories: **160** | Total fat: **6g** | Saturated fat: **2g** | Sodium: **157mg** | Carbs: **1g** | Fiber: **0g** | Protein: **24g**

CITRUSY MEXICAN PULLED PORK

Prep time: **15 minutes** | Cook time: **4 hours on high or 8 hours on low** | Serves **6**

- 1 tablespoon dried oregano
- 2 teaspoons ground cumin
- 2 teaspoons garlic powder
- 2 teaspoons onion powder
- ¼ teaspoon cayenne pepper
- 2 pounds boneless pork loin, trimmed of fat
- ½ onion, chopped
- 3 garlic cloves, minced
- 1 jalapeño pepper, seeded and chopped
- juice of 1 lime
- juice of 1 orange

1. Combine the oregano, cumin, garlic powder, onion powder, and cayenne in a small bowl. Rub this mixture over the entire surface of the pork loin. Place the pork into a 4- to 6-quart slow cooker.
2. Top the pork with the onion, minced garlic, jalapeño, lime juice, and orange juice. Cover and cook on high for 4 hours or on low for 8 hours.
3. Remove the pork and shred it using two forks. Return the shredded pork to the slow cooker to soak up the liquid and to keep hot before serving.

Per Serving

Calories: **243** | Total Fat: **11g** | Saturated Fat: **4g** | Carbs: **7g** | Fiber: **2g** | Sugars: **3g** | Protein: **29g**

MARINATED STEAK

Prep time: **10 minutes** | Cook time: **5 minutes** | Serves **6**

- ⅔ cup dry red wine (regular or nonalcoholic)
- 2 teaspoons dry sherry
- 1 teaspoon soy sauce (lowest sodium available)
- ⅛ teaspoon dried oregano, crumbled
- ⅛ teaspoon dried marjoram, crumbled
- ⅛ teaspoon grated peeled gingerroot
- ⅛ teaspoon toasted sesame oil
- Pepper to taste (freshly ground preferred)
- 1 ½ pounds flank steak, all visible fat and silver skin discarded

1. In a large shallow glass dish, whisk together the marinade ingredients. Add the beef, turning to coat. Cover and refrigerate for at least 12 to 18 hours, turning occasionally.
2. Preheat the broiler. Drain the beef, discarding the marinade.
3. Broil 4 to 6 inches from the heat for 5 minutes on each side. Transfer to a cutting board. Thinly slice the beef diagonally across the grain.

Per Serving

Calories: **158** | Total Fat: **6.5 g** | Saturated Fat: **3.0 g** | Carbs: **0 gg** | Fiber: **0 g** | Sugars: **0 g** | Protein: **23 g**

RED BEANS, SAUSAGE, AND RICE

Prep time: 20 minutes | **Cook time: 30 minutes** | Serves **4**

- ¾ cup uncooked parboiled brown rice or 2 cups cooked brown rice
- 1 tablespoon canola or sunflower oil
- 6 ounces smoked andouille sausage, cut into bite-size pieces
- 1 onion, chopped
- 1 green bell pepper, seeded and chopped
- 1 red bell pepper, seeded and chopped
- 4 garlic cloves, minced
- 1 (28-ounce) can no-salt-added whole tomatoes
- 1 (15-ounce) can no-salt-added kidney beans, rinsed and drained
- 1 teaspoon ground cumin
- 1 teaspoon dried thyme
- ½ teaspoon red pepper flakes
- ¼ teaspoon freshly ground black pepper

1. Start the rice cooking according to the package directions.
2. Meanwhile, heat the oil in a large, heavy skillet over medium-high heat. Add the sausage and cook until lightly browned, 3 to 4 minutes. Add the onion, bell peppers, and garlic, and cook until softened, 5 to 6 minutes.
3. Stir in the tomatoes with their juice, beans, cumin, thyme, red pepper flakes, and black pepper. Bring to a boil. Add the rice whether it's ready or not (including any water yet to be absorbed). Turn the heat down to medium-low, and cover. Simmer until the rice is fully cooked, 5 to 10 minutes.
4. Taste, and adjust the seasonings.

Per Serving

Calories: 395 | **Total Fat: 11g** | **Saturated Fat: 3g** | **Carbs: 58g** | **Fiber: 15g** | **Added Sugars: 0g** | **Protein: 20g**

CHAPTER 10: VEGGIE VENTURE

EGGPLANT AND CHICKPEA STEW

Prep time: 15 minutes | Cook time: 50 minutes | Serves 6

- 1½ pounds eggplant, diced
- ½ teaspoon salt, divided
- 2 tablespoons extra-virgin olive oil
- 1 onion, chopped
- 2 (15-ounce) cans low-sodium chickpeas, drained and rinsed
- 1 (28-ounce) can low-sodium diced tomatoes
- 2 cups water, plus more as needed
- 2 teaspoons paprika
- ½ teaspoon freshly ground black pepper
- crusty bread, for serving

1. Put the eggplant in a colander, and sprinkle with ¼ teaspoon of salt. Let rest for 10 minutes, then press to extract as much water as possible.
2. In a large pot, heat the oil over medium-high heat.
3. Add the onion, and sauté for 3 to 5 minutes, or until browned.
4. Add the eggplant, chickpeas, tomatoes with their juices, water, paprika, pepper, and remaining ¼ teaspoon of salt.
5. Reduce the heat to medium-low. Cover the pot, and simmer for 30 to 45 minutes, or until the eggplant is tender. Open the lid and stir the mixture a couple times as it cooks, adding more water, ½ cup at a time, to form a sauce. Remove from the heat.

Per Serving

Calories: **206** | Total fat: **7g** | Saturated fat: **1g** | Sodium: **365mg** | Carbs: **31g** | Fiber: **10g** | Protein: **8g** | Calcium: **62mg**

VEGGIE LASAGNA

Prep time: 15 minutes | Cook time: 6½ to 7½ hours on low | Serves 6

- nonstick cooking spray
- 4 cups rustic marinara sauce, divided
- 8 whole-wheat lasagna noodles
- 1½ cups part-skim ricotta cheese, divided
- ¾ cup green peas, thawed if frozen, divided
- 3 cups baby spinach, divided
- 3 cups sliced zucchini, divided
- 1 cup frozen butternut squash purée, thawed, divided
- 3 portobello mushroom caps, gills removed and thinly sliced, divided
- ½ cup shredded part-skim mozzarella cheese, divided

1. Lightly spray the inside of a 6-quart slow cooker with the cooking spray. Spread ½ cup of marinara sauce on the bottom of the slow cooker. Add a layer of noodles, trying not to overlap them. Break them into pieces, if necessary, to fully cover the bottom.
2. Cover the noodles with ½ cup of ricotta cheese, ¼ cup of green peas, 1 cup of spinach, 1 cup of zucchini, ⅓ cup of squash purée, 1 sliced mushroom, and ¾ cup of marinara sauce. Repeat these layers twice more for three layers total. End with a final layer of noodles, the remaining ¼ cup of marinara sauce, and the mozzarella cheese.
3. Cover and cook on low for 6 to 7 hours. Then turn the slow cooker off and let the lasagna set for 30 minutes before serving to allow the noodles to firm up.
4. Serve hot.

Per Serving

Calories: **364** | Total Fat: **11g** | Saturated Fat: **5g** | Carbs: **48g** | Fiber: **10g** | Sugars: **10g** | Protein: **20g**

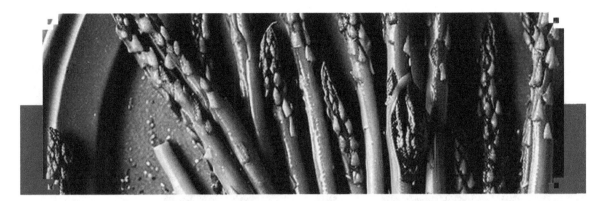

NATURE'S VEGGIE BURGER

Prep time: 15 minutes | Cook time: 25 minutes | Serves 4

- 3 tablespoons extra-virgin olive oil
- 1 tablespoon chopped garlic
- 4 very large portobello mushrooms, gills and stems removed
- 4 crusty whole-grain rolls or 1 multigrain baguette cut into 3-inch-long pieces
- ½ cup crumbled goat cheese
- freshly ground black pepper (optional)
- 4 green lettuce leaves

1. Preheat a grill to medium. (Alternatively, preheat the oven to 425°F and line a rimmed baking sheet with aluminum foil.)
2. Mix the olive oil and the chopped garlic in a small bowl. Brush about half of the mixture on both sides of the mushrooms, and let them sit for 10 minutes.
3. Meanwhile, split open the rolls. Drizzle the remaining garlic-infused oil onto the bottom half of each roll, including the garlic if you like. Spread about 2 tablespoons of goat cheese on the top half of each roll.
4. Place the mushrooms on the grill, cap-side down, close the lid, and grill until they're brown and tender, 5 to 10 minutes, turning once. (Or place them on the foil-lined sheet, cap-side down, and roast in the oven for 12 minutes on each side.)
5. Put one mushroom on the bottom of each roll. Add a grind of pepper, if desired. Top with a leaf of lettuce and then the top of the roll.

Per Serving

Calories: **307** | Total Fat: **17g** | Saturated Fat: **5g** | Carbs: **26g** | Fiber: **4g** | **Added** Sugars: **0g** | Protein: **6g**

LEMON-ROASTED ASPARAGUS

Prep time: 10 minutes | Cook time: 15 minutes | Serves 2

- 1 bunch asparagus, trimmed 1 inch from the bottom (20 or 30 spears)
- 2 teaspoons avocado oil
- 2 teaspoons lemon zest
- 2 tablespoons lemon juice
- 2 garlic cloves, minced
- ½ teaspoon freshly ground black pepper

1. Preheat the oven to 425°F. Line a baking sheet with parchment paper and lay out the asparagus.
2. Mix the oil, lemon zest, lemon juice, garlic, and pepper and toss with the asparagus until well coated.
3. Bake for 12 to 15 minutes, until the asparagus is fork-tender and the tops are crispy. This dish can be stored in an airtight container for up to 5 days, but is best served warm.

Per Serving

Calories: **90** | Total fat: **5g** | Saturated fat: **1g** | Carbs: **10g** | Sugars: **4g** | Fiber: **5g** | Protein: **5g**

GREEN BEANS SAUTÉ

Prep time: **5 minutes** | Cook time: **15 minutes** | Serves **4**

- 1 lb fresh or frozen green beans, cut in 1-inch pieces
- 1 tbsp vegetable oil
- 1 large yellow onion, halved lengthwise, thinly sliced
- ½ tsp salt
- ⅛ tsp black pepper
- 1 tbsp fresh parsley, minced

1. If using fresh green beans, cook in boiling water for 10 to 12 minutes or steam for 2 to 3 minutes until barely fork tender. Drain well. If using frozen green beans, thaw first.
2. Heat oil in large skillet. Sauté onion until golden.
3. Stir in green beans, salt, and pepper. Heat through.
4. Before serving, toss with parsley.

Per Serving:

Calories: **64**| Total Fat: **4g**| Total Fiber: **3g**| Protein: **2g**| Carbs: **8g**

BLACK BEAN QUESADILLAS

Prep time: **25 minutes** | Cook time: **25 minutes** | Serves **4**

- 1 (15-ounce) can no-salt-added black beans, rinsed and drained
- ¼ cup fresh tomato salsa or lower-sodium store-bought salsa
- ¾ cup shredded cheddar cheese, divided
- 1 red bell pepper, seeded and chopped, divided
- 2 tablespoons canola or sunflower oil, divided
- 4 large, whole-grain tortillas

1. Blend the beans and salsa together in a food processor. If you don't have a food processor, mash them in a large bowl with a fork or a potato masher.
2. Spread one-fourth of the bean mixture (about ½ cup) on each tortilla. Sprinkle each with 3 tablespoons of cheese and one-fourth of the bell pepper (about ¼ cup). Fold in half.
3. Preheat a large, heavy skillet over medium heat. Add 1 tablespoon of oil to the skillet and spread it around. Place the first two quesadillas in the skillet. Cover and cook until the quesadillas are crispy on the bottom, about 2 minutes. Flip and cook until crispy on the other side, about 2 minutes more.
4. Use the remaining 1 tablespoon of oil to cook the remaining two quesadillas, keeping the first two warm in the oven if needed.

Per Serving

Calories: **438** | Total Fat: **21g** | Saturated Fat: **5g** | Carbs: **46g** | Fiber: **12g** | Added Sugars: **0g** | Protein: **17g**

EDAMAME AND CARROT TAHINI FALAFEL BALLS

Prep time: **10 minutes** | Cook time: **15 minutes** | Serves **4**

- 2 medium carrots, peeled and cut into 1-inch chunks
- 2 cups edamame (fully cooked and shelled)
- ½ cup old-fashioned rolled oats
- ⅓ cup unsalted tahini
- 1 teaspoon za'atar (see tip)
- ½ cup chopped fresh basil
- ¼ teaspoon freshly ground black pepper

1. Preheat the oven to 400°F. Line a baking sheet with parchment paper.
2. Put the carrots in a blender or food processor and pulse for 30 seconds until pulverized. Add the edamame, oats, tahini, za'atar, basil, and pepper and blend until combined, about 1 minute, scraping down the sides halfway through. The texture should be doughy, but sticky enough to form into balls.
3. Form the mixture into 2-ounce balls and place on the lined baking sheet. Flatten them slightly with the back of a fork so they can be easily flipped.
4. Bake for 10 minutes, then flip when lightly golden. Bake for another 5 minutes until the other side is lightly golden and crispy. Serve warm with desired toppings or store in an airtight container in the refrigerator for up to 5 days.

Per Serving

Calories: **271** | Total fat: **15g** | Saturated fat: **2g** | Carbs: **23g** | Sugars: **3g** | Fiber: **7g** | Protein: **15g**

RANCH-STYLE PINTO BEANS

Prep time: **10 minutes, plus overnight to soak** | Cook time: **7 to 8 hours on low** | Serves **8**

- 1 pound dried pinto beans, soaked overnight
- 5 cups beef stock or low-sodium beef broth
- 1 cup low-sodium tomato sauce
- 1 medium white onion, diced
- 1 jalapeño pepper, seeded, and finely diced
- 4 garlic cloves, minced
- 1 tablespoon ancho chili powder
- 1 teaspoon chili powder
- 1 teaspoon apple cider vinegar
- 1 teaspoon ground cumin
- 1 packed teaspoon brown sugar
- 1 teaspoon smoked paprika
- ½ teaspoon dried oregano
- freshly ground black pepper

1. Drain and rinse the soaked beans. Put them in a 6-quart slow cooker along with the stock, tomato sauce, onion, jalapeño, garlic, ancho chili powder, chili powder, vinegar, cumin, sugar, paprika, and oregano.
2. Cover and cook on low for 7 to 8 hours, until the beans are tender and the liquid has thickened slightly.
3. Taste and season with the pepper. Serve warm.

Per Serving

Calories: **222** | Total Fat: **0g** | Saturated Fat: **0g** | Carbs: **40g** | Fiber: **8g** | Sugars: **3g** | Protein: **14g**

CHAPTER 11: SWEET FINALE

YOGURT CHEESECAKE

Prep time: 10 minutes | Cook time: 35 minutes | Serves 4

- 1¼ cups fat-free Greek yogurt
- 2 tablespoons arrowroot starch
- 1½ egg whites
- ½ cup cocoa powder
- ½ teaspoon organic vanilla extract

1. Preheat the baking oven to 350° F and grease a cake pan.
2. Meanwhile, add everything in a bowl and mix well.
3. Pour the mixture in the cake pan and bake for about 35 minutes.
4. Take out and set aside to cool.
5. Refrigerate for three to four hours, slice and serve.

Per Serving

Calories: 180 | Fat: 5.6g | Sat Fat: 3.3g | Carbs: 26.8g | Fiber: 3.3g | Sugar: 16.4g | Protein: 11.7g

SWEET POTATO AND SQUASH PIE

Prep time: 10 minutes | Cook time: 1 hour | Serves 8

- 1 sweet potato (about ¼ lb.), peeled and cooked
- 1 buttercup squash (about 2½ lbs.), peeled, seeded, and cooked
- ½ cup silken tofu
- ½ cup soy milk
- ¼ cup egg whites
- ¼ cup rye flour
- ½ tsp. each clove, cinnamon, nutmeg, and vanilla extract
- 1 tsp. freshly grated ginger
- 1 tsp. orange zest
- 3 tbsp. honey
- 1 frozen pre-made 9-inch pie shell

1. Heat the oven to 300˚F.
2. Puree the sweet potato and squash in a food processor. Place in a large bowl.
3. Add the remaining ingredients and mix together until smooth and well-combined.
4. Place the pie shell on a sheet pan. Pour the mixture into the pie shell and bake for 45 to 55 minutes or until the internal temperature is 180˚F.

Per Serving

Calories: 210 | Protein: 5g | Carbs: 34g | Fiber: 4g | Fat: 6g | Sodium: 109mg

STRAWBERRY-RASPBERRY ICE

Prep time: **10 minutes** | Cook time: **15 minutes** | Serves 8

- 6 ounces frozen 100% white grape juice concentrate
- 1 cup water
- 2 tablespoons confectioners' sugar
- 8 ounces frozen unsweetened strawberries, slightly thawed
- 6 ounces frozen unsweetened raspberries, slightly thawed
- 6 ice cubes (about 1 cup), slightly chopped
- Sprigs of fresh mint (optional)

1. In a food processor or blender, combine all the ingredients except the mint in the order listed. Process until smooth (except for the seeds), stirring occasionally. Pour into a large resealable plastic freezer bag and seal tightly. Place the bag on its side in the freezer and let the mixture freeze solid, at least 2 hours.
2. About 15 minutes before serving, remove the bag from the freezer and let the ice thaw slightly, mashing with a fork if necessary. At serving time, spoon into chilled glasses. Garnish with the mint sprigs. Serve immediately.

Per Serving

Calories: **91** | Total Fat: **0.0 g** | Saturated Fat: **0.0 g** | Carbs: **23 gg** | Fiber: **2 g** | Sugars: **19 g** | Protein: **0 g**

PEACH AND BLUEBERRY TART

Prep time: **10 minutes** | Cook time: **30 minutes** | Serves 6–8

- 1 sheet frozen puff pastry
- 1 cup fresh blueberries
- 4 peaches, pitted and sliced
- 3 tablespoons sugar
- 2 tablespoons cornstarch
- 1 tablespoon freshly squeezed lemon juice
- cooking spray
- 1 tablespoon nonfat or low-fat milk
- confectioners' sugar, for dusting

1. Thaw puff pastry at room temperature for at least 30 minutes.
2. Preheat the oven to 400°F.
3. In a large bowl, toss the blueberries, peaches, sugar, cornstarch, and lemon juice.
4. Spray a round pie pan with cooking spray.
5. Unfold pastry and place on prepared pie pan.
6. Arrange the peach slices so they are slightly overlapping. Spread the blueberries on top of the peaches.
7. Drape pastry over the outside of the fruit and press pleats firmly together. Brush with milk.
8. Bake in the bottom third of the oven until crust is golden, about 30 minutes.
9. Cool on a rack.
10. Sprinkle pastry with confectioners' sugar. Serve.

Per Serving

Total Calories: **119** | Total Fat: **3g** | Saturated Fat: **1g** | Total Carbs: **23g** | Fiber: **2g** | Sugars: **15g** | Protein: **1g**

CHOCOLATE MOUSSE

Prep time: **5 minutes** | Cook time: **10 minutes** | Serves **6**

- 1 (3.5-ounce) bar 70-percent dark chocolate
- 1 (14-ounce) package extra-firm tofu, excess water drained and tofu patted dry
- 1 teaspoon pure vanilla extract
- 1 teaspoon honey
- 1 teaspoon cinnamon

1. In a medium microwave-safe bowl, heat the chocolate bar in the microwave in 30-second increments until the bar has melted, about 2 minutes.
2. In a blender, blend the tofu, vanilla, honey, cinnamon, and melted chocolate until smooth, about 1 minute, scraping down the sides as needed. Serve as is.
3. The mousse can be stored in an airtight container in the refrigerator for up to 3 days. The mixture may thicken slightly as it cools.

Per Serving

Calories: **131** | Total fat: **18g** | Saturated fat: **4g** | Carbs: **9g** | Sugars: **5g** | Fiber: **2g** | Protein: **6g**

ALMOND RICE PUDDING

Prep time: **10 minutes** | Cook time: **10 minutes** | Serves **6**

- 3 cups fat-free milk
- 1 cup white rice
- ¼ cup sugar
- 1 tsp. vanilla
- ¼ tsp. almond extract
- cinnamon to taste
- ¼ cup toasted almonds
- cherry compote to garnish

1. Mix rice and milk in a medium baking dish.
2. At 350°F, preheat your air fryer.
3. Cook the pudding in the air fryer for 10 minutes.
4. Allow the pudding to cool, then stir in the rest of the ingredients.
5. Garnish with cherry compote and refrigerate for 3 hours.
6. Serve.

Per Serving

Calories: **220** | Fat: **3.4g** | Carbs: **40.1g** | Protein: **7.2g** | Cholesterol: **6mg** | Sodium: **55mg** | Fiber: **3g**

COFFEE AND CREAM SORBET

Prep time: **10 minutes** | Cook time: **none** | Serves **6**

- 1 ½ cups strong dark coffee, warmed
- ¼ cup light corn syrup
- 2 tablespoons fat-free half-and-half
- 1 tablespoon coffee liqueur (optional)

1. In a medium bowl, whisk together the coffee and corn syrup until the corn syrup is dissolved. Cover and refrigerate until cold.
2. Stir the half-and-half and liqueur into the coffee mixture.
3. Pour the coffee mixture into an ice cream maker. Freeze according to the manufacturer's directions.
4. At serving time, spoon ⅓ cup sorbet into sherbet or parfait glasses.

Per Serving

Calories: **45** | Total Fat: **0.0 g** | Saturated Fat: **0.0 g** | Carbs: **12 gg** | Fiber: **0 g** | Sugars: **12 g** | Protein: **0 g**

MIXED BERRY COFFEE CAKE

Prep time: **15 minutes** | Cook time: **30 minutes** | Serves **6**

- ½ cup skim milk
- 1 tablespoon vinegar
- 2 tablespoons canola oil
- 1 teaspoon vanilla
- 1 egg
- ⅓ cup packed brown sugar
- 1 cup whole-wheat pastry flour
- ½ teaspoon baking soda
- ½ teaspoon ground cinnamon
- ⅛ teaspoon salt
- 1 cup frozen mixed berries
- ¼ cup low-fat granola, crushed

1. Preheat the oven to 350°F.
2. Grease an 8-inch baking pan with cooking spray and then dust it with flour.
3. Combine the milk with the vanilla, oil, vinegar, brown sugar, and egg until smooth.
4. Add the baking soda, cinnamon, salt, and flour. Mix well.
5. Fold in half of the berries and transfer the batter to the pan.
6. Top it with the remaining berries and the granola.
7. Bake for 30 minutes until golden brown.
8. Serve.

Per Serving

Calories: **135** | Fat: **23g** | Sodium **50mg** | Carbs: **22g** | Fiber: **3g** | Sugar: **4g** | Protein: **4g**

MEASUREMENT CONVERSION CHART

VOLUME EQUIVALENTS(DRY)

US STANDARD	METRIC (APPROXIMATE)
1/8 teaspoon	0.5 mL
1/4 teaspoon	1 mL
1/2 teaspoon	2 mL
3/4 teaspoon	4 mL
1 teaspoon	5 mL
1 tablespoon	15 mL
1/4 cup	59 mL
1/2 cup	118 mL
3/4 cup	177 mL
1 cup	235 mL
2 cups	475 mL
3 cups	700 mL
4 cups	1 L

WEIGHT EQUIVALENTS

US STANDARD	METRIC (APPROXIMATE)
1 ounce	28 g
2 ounces	57 g
5 ounces	142 g
10 ounces	284 g
15 ounces	425 g
16 ounces (1 pound)	455 g
1.5 pounds	680 g
2 pounds	907 g

VOLUME EQUIVALENTS(LIQUID)

US STANDARD	US STANDARD (OUNCES)	METRIC (APPROXIMATE)
2 tablespoons	1 fl.oz.	30 mL
1/4 cup	2 fl.oz.	60 mL
1/2 cup	4 fl.oz.	120 mL
1 cup	8 fl.oz.	240 mL
1 1/2 cup	12 fl.oz.	355 mL
2 cups or 1 pint	16 fl.oz.	475 mL
4 cups or 1 quart	32 fl.oz.	1 L
1 gallon	128 fl.oz.	4 L

TEMPERATURES EQUIVALENTS

FAHRENHEIT(F)	CELSIUS(C) (APPROXIMATE)
225 °F	107 °C
250 °F	120 °C
275 °F	135 °C
300 °F	150 °C
325 °F	160 °C
350 °F	180 °C
375 °F	190 °C
400 °F	205 °C
425 °F	220 °C
450 °F	235 °C
475 °F	245 °C
500 °F	260 °C

The Dirty Dozen and Clean Fifteen

The Environmental Working Group (EWG) is a nonprofit, nonpartisan organization dedicated to protecting human health and the environment Its mission is to empower people to live healthier lives in a healthier environment. This organization publishes an annual list of the twelve kinds of produce, in sequence, that have the highest amount of pesticide residue-the Dirty Dozen-as well as a list of the fifteen kinds ofproduce that have the least amount of pesticide residue-the Clean Fifteen.

THE DIRTY DOZEN

- The 2016 Dirty Dozen includes the following produce. These are considered among the year's most important produce to buy organic:

Strawberries	Spinach
Apples	Tomatoes
Nectarines	Bell peppers
Peaches	Cherry tomatoes
Celery	Cucumbers
Grapes	Kale/collard greens
Cherries	Hot peppers

- *The Dirty Dozen list contains two additional itemskale/collard greens and hot peppers-because they tend to contain trace levels of highly hazardous pesticides.*

THE CLEAN FIFTEEN

- The least critical to buy organically are the Clean Fifteen list. The following are on the 2016 list:

Avocados	Papayas
Corn	Kiw
Pineapples	Eggplant
Cabbage	Honeydew
Sweet peas	Grapefruit
Onions	Cantaloupe
Asparagus	Cauliflower
Mangos	

- *Some of the sweet corn sold in the United States are made from genetically engineered (GE) seedstock. Buy organic varieties of these crops to avoid GE produce.*

APPENDIX 3: INDEX

Hey there!

Wow, can you believe we've reached the end of this culinary journey together? I'm truly thrilled and filled with joy as I think back on all the recipes we've shared and the flavors we've discovered. This experience, blending a bit of tradition with our own unique twists, has been a journey of love for good food. And knowing you've been out there, giving these dishes a try, has made this adventure incredibly special to me.

Even though we're turning the last page of this book, I hope our conversation about all things delicious doesn't have to end. I cherish your thoughts, your experiments, and yes, even those moments when things didn't go as planned. Every piece of feedback you share is invaluable, helping to enrich this experience for us all.

I'd be so grateful if you could take a moment to share your thoughts with me, be it through a review on Amazon or any other place you feel comfortable expressing yourself online. Whether it's praise, constructive criticism, or even an idea for how we might do things differently in the future, your input is what truly makes this journey meaningful.

This book is a piece of my heart, offered to you with all the love and enthusiasm I have for cooking. But it's your engagement and your words that elevate it to something truly extraordinary.

Thank you from the bottom of my heart for being such an integral part of this culinary adventure. Your openness to trying new things and sharing your experiences has been the greatest gift.

Catch you later,

Wendy C. Thomas

Made in the USA
Las Vegas, NV
26 December 2024

15401912R00044